From The Times 1975
Mr N
her

BY CHANCE
I DID ROVE

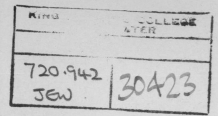
ISBN 0 948041 01 3
Copyright 1986 Nancy Jewson

1st published (privately) 1951
2nd edition 1973
This edition Gryffon Publications 1986

ACKNOWLEDGEMENTS

The publisher would like to offer special thanks
to Mr. David Gould for his introduction and to
Mrs. F. L. Griggs for allowing the use of her
late husband's drawings.
Thanks are also due to Miss Nancy Jewson,
Mrs Anthony Biddulph, Mrs. Laurie Clark,
Mr. Bill Hughes, Cheltenham Art Gallery & Museums
and the Museum of English Rural Life, Reading,
for assistance and for the loan of photographs.

The original dedication of this book
was to Lilias, Countess Bathurst

Printed and published by Davina Wynne - Jones
Gryffon Publications, Turk's Yard, Barnsley,
Nr. Cirencester, Gloucestershire GL7 5EF

[ii]

BY CHANCE
I DID ROVE

by Norman Jewson

WITH AN
INTRODUCTION BY
DAVID GOULD

Gryffon Publications 1986

ILLUSTRATIONS

CONTENTS

INTRODUCTION

THESE charming reminiscences by Norman Jewson were first published in a limited edition of 250 copies in 1951 for circulation among his friends. In the same year, from May until September, there was an exhibition *The Cotswold Tradition* at Cirencester. This was organized mainly by Oliver Hill, the architect, and John Betjeman, and it helped to bring about a revival of interest in the district, with special reference to the architectural work and furniture designs of Ernest Gimson and his friends. Norman Jewson worked with Gimson from 1907 until Gimson's untimely death in 1919, and he knew everybody connected with the group. He was steeped in the *new* Cotswold tradition, which might be called an offshoot of the Arts and Crafts Movement, and in his book he gives some charming vignettes not only of the architects and craftsmen but also of the delightful and happy village life at Sapperton from mid-Edwardian days until the late 1920's. He wrote with that engaging simplicity and directness which John Aubrey, the Wiltshire antiquary, called "the art of local memory."

Much to Norman's surprise, the small edition of his book was soon exhausted, and it became somewhat of a rarity. The references to Gimson and the Barnsleys made it one of the few 'source' books for anyone interested in the Cotswold crafts. But it was over twenty years later, in 1973, before a new and illustrated edition was suggested, with thirteen monochrome plates and ten line illustrations—a well produced edition which gave Norman much pleasure. His little book had survived and it was still appreciated. He was by now 87 years of age. He was flattered to have the reproductions of his own drawings as well as photographs of the places he loved and had written about, and with the old photographs of the Victorian worthies of Sapperton.

That another edition of the book should now be called for shows the ever growing interest in the Cotswolds during the last twelve years. Certain factors have given this truly enchanting book an enduring quality. It is written with an engaging simplicity which makes it the sort of book which people feel they themselves might have written with ease, for everyone, sooner or later, has an idea that they have a book in them. Norman's style is so simple and so direct that a sense of reality is never absent. It is a long way from the polished Cambridge style that one might expect from a graduate of Gonville and Caius. But Norman, although exceedingly well read, managed to keep himself uncluttered by civilization, and his writing reflected this. I can hear him speaking when I read his words, his book is like a conversation, as if he is gently answering questions.

It is unusual for a minor work of English rural literature to be reprinted at all, let alone reprinted *yet again* some thirty-five years after it first came out. Hundreds of books dealing with aspects of rural history, each of immense interest to a particular locality, seem to have been published in the last hundred years, and many minor masterpieces are to be found among them. In themselves they form a fascinating subject for study. To the forefront comes Atkinson's *Forty Years in a Moorland Parish*, which is surely one of the finest works in this genre ever to have been issued, with Miss Ashby's *The Changing English Village* also high in the list. And who could ever forget Frederick Brittain's *Tales of South Mymms and Elsewhere*, with the memorable portrayal of the incapacitated countryman

Feeny Arnold?

A brief survey of such published works take far more space than this preface allows, beginning with early translations of Virgil and coming eventually to the numerous effusions of the last hundred years or so. Each reader will have a preferred list of memorable writers, from Cobbett, George Sturt, Alfred Williams, the Hammonds, the 'Son of the Marshes' (Owen), Jefferies, Hudson, Hoskins and Finberg, etc. In fact, it seems as if there is an almost inexhaustible list of books about old English life and the English countryside, to which may be added an amazingly vast quantity of unpublished material. For example, at the time of the Golden Jubilee of the Women's Institute Movement, in 1973, it was suggested to some nine thousand villages that they should celebrate this by compiling scrapbooks and making written records of village life. Some 2,600 responded, and their productions are now housed in the care of County archivists and local libraries.

One of the saddest aspects of rural literature is the picture of abject poverty so often depicted. Owing in the main to agricultural depression, the peasantry often lived under the most appalling conditions, eeking out their dreary lives on a diet of bread and lard. Norman Jewson was acutely aware of the discrepancy between the haves and the have nots in the sixty years between 1880 and 1940, but he does not dwell at length upon them. He was very sensitive about the problem, and, like F. E. Green, found the glamour of the picturesque was all too soon unmasked. Green's book *The Tyranny of the Countryside*, published in 1913, is a searching enquiry into the decay of cottages. In the Cotswolds thousands of acres were lying idle. "Poverty haunts the dark alleys of the broad high street of mediaeval Chipping Campden," he wrote, "where the musty old-world atmosphere pervades the whole town."

When Norman announced that he preferred this poetic
but impoverished and yet beautiful countryside to the
middle-class security of Norwich and the family timber
business, he was dramatically cut off by his family and
left to make his own way. And this he did very success-
fully, firstly with Gimson and afterwards in his own
office and architect's practise in Cirencester. He lived in
Gloucestershire for nearly seventy years. He was at
Frampton Mansell for a short while before moving to
Sapperton, where he had a small cottage on the lower
road to the Church before moving to the bigger cottage
which he describes, and the subsequent enlargement
when the two minute adjacent cottages became vacant.
The little house, set behind a yew arch, with tall yews
meticulously clipped as 'cheeses' of diminishing sizes and
surmounted by yew peacocks which were trimmed once a
year, was set upon high ground facing the Green. He
told me that the yews had hardly altered from generation
to generation. The front garden was always filled with
roses. Low box hedges, no more than twelve inches
high, edged the regular and geometric beds. The walls
of the cottage were covered with vines and clematis, and
morning glory and passion flowers were abundant,
framing the windows where Mary Jewson's many and
varied cactii sat incongruously along the inside cills.

In Norman's eyes Sapperton was an Arcadian place.
Ernest Gimson made it so. He describes how he
accompanied Gimson on his long walks each day, and
gathered wisdom and knowledge from him. Gimson
had a passion for the countryside, and for country things
and for country people. With his wife Emmie they
organised village dances and innocent amusements at
Sapperton, and to start with there was much happiness
in the community. But it was not to last. The 1914
to 1918 war was a great divide, and the atmosphere of
the 'liberated' 1920's was no longer conducive to the

quiet country ways.

Gimson's influence was immediately seen inside Norman's house. It was uncluttered, bearing in mind Morris's maxim not to have anything which was not beautiful or useful. Yet it was very comfortably furnished with antique furniture and with pieces of oak designed by his father-in-law Ernest Barnsley and by Gimson. The curtains and the chintzes were by William Morris, and the snow white walls, which were regularly painted, were hung with delightful water-colours of flowers by Edith Payne and with landscapes of Cotswold scenes by Henry Payne, Russell Alexander, and by Fred Griggs. Some of Norman's own water-colours, mainly of Italian scenes, were hung in the dining room. On the mantleshelf above the wide log fire in the sitting-room were two water-colours of his daughters. Between them stood a Staffordshire group called *The Tithe*. It depicted the Parson holding a suckling-pig, and next to him stood a young girl holding a baby. This was a never ending source of amusement to him. As a contrast there was, on the top of his bureau, a very fine early Chinese ivory tusk carving of Shou Lao, the God of Longevity, with his enormous brow, quietly contemplating the passing world through heavy-lidded eyes. There was china decorated by Grace Barnsley on the oak sideboard and dresser, and there was some enchanting plasterwork of his own design, which children always found magical, depicting rabbits, hares, an owl, a hedgehog and tiny bunches of little daisies—batchelor's buttons (was not the group of cottages which he converted into his house originally called 'Batchelor's Court?').

The hearth was the centre of the house, with the ever pervasive and delightful aroma of woodsmoke—even if it did alter the colour of the vellum bindings. His own collection of books was small, and it was strictly limited to those he really liked and often re-read. These included a well-thumbed *Life of Samuel Palmer*, and fine editions of Palmer's own versions of *Milton* and of *Virgil*, and a well-handled copy of the Shakespeare Head Press book about *Ernest Gimson*. He liked the works of Browne and Burton, and many of the Old Authors. He would read and re-read the Poems by his friend Russell Alexander. He had the Gospels bound in full—and more than somewhat grimy—pigskin, with the decorations by Eric Gill. At ceiling height, and along the beams of his sitting room were oak shelves lined with books, a way of keeping them originally devised by Gimson. These were mainly poets which he had re-bound or re-cased himself in full or quarter vellum with the boards covered in decorative Italian papers which he bought each time he went to Florence. Most of these had turned reddish-brown, 'kippered', as he called it, from the woodsmoke of his capacious hearth. Since his death the large and very solid oak settle, which was originally Gimson's and which dominated the living room, has gone to Owlpen Manor, and his print cabinet and bookcase have gone to the sculptor Simon Verity, who lived at Daneway House for a while in the early 1970's with his uncle, Oliver Hill, and spent many happy hours visiting Sapperton, just across the valley.

To outward appearances Norman Jewson was a distinguished looking man, tall and, until his very last years, bolt upright. There was no questioning but that he was essentially a countryman—a man who seemed utterly out of place walking along a London road. I once caught sight of him quite by chance during one of his rare visits to London. He was staying with friends on Hammersmith Terrace: and it was on the busy approach road to Hammersmith Bridge that I saw him, stick in hand, walking for all the world as if he was just striding along one of the broad 'rides' in Cirencester Park, on the way to 'Cissiter.' All around him the Londoners were bustling along with their heads down. He alone was walking with his head held high, 'looking at the birds.'

Blessed with an old world charm, he had many dear friends. Indeed, he had a gift for friendship; always courteous and kind, always interested in country matters, always willing to pass the time of day with anyone he met on his long rambles around the countryside. Chief among his friends were the etcher Fred Griggs and the journalist Russell Alexander, who spent his nights churning out copy for a London daily paper and his days, when he had time, writing many delightful verses. The three friends always tried to have an annual jaunt together, a holiday jollification, a sketching tour searching for 'bits of old England', when they would be endlessly planning and writing essays and poems, and dreaming about books to be written. It is much to be regretted that Norman never expanded his reminiscences. And it is equally to be regretted that Russell Alexander never had time to settle down to write his long expected biography of Griggs, since he, alone, was the most appropriate person to have done the job. Alas! Shortly after a long awaited retirement, he died in his new cottage home in Wiltshire. In the past twenty-five years there has been a gradual revival of interest in the work of Gimson, and in the Arts and Crafts Movement in general. The genius of F. L. Griggs is again recognised and his work has many admirers. I hope the time will soon come when it will be possible to edit and publish some of the many delightful letters which passed between Griggs and Russell Alexander and Norman Jewson, for they had a multitude of good things in common.

David Gould, 1986

Cirencester Church Porch by F. L. Griggs

[*xiv*]

Chapter I

FIRST SIGHT OF THE COTSWOLDS

WHEN I stepped out of the train at Cirencester station one fine day in August 1907, I little thought that, apart from a few short intervals, the Cotswolds were to be my home for the next forty years.* For the previous three years I had been articled to Herbert Ibberson, a charming man and a talented architect, working at his office in Lincoln's Inn. Now that my apprenticeship was finished I was starting on a holiday in a part of the country little known at that time, except to a few architects and artists who had discovered its fine stone buildings and varied and beautiful scenery. Hitherto my life had been spent almost entirely in East Anglia. Born at Norwich, at school in Norfolk and Suffolk, then three years at Cambridge, followed by another three in London, which I disliked as a place to live in permanently the longer I stayed there, though I recognised its advantages in other ways, I was looking forward to an escape from town life to a part of the country that was new to me and which had the added attraction of a fine stone architecture to study.

Cirencester, as I knew from a book I had brought with me, had been described as 'the capital of the Cotswolds', so my plan was to start from there in any direction, in search of the subjects for my sketch book, which I hoped to find in almost every village. I had brought a small tent with me, with a few books and spare clothes, intending to buy some simple cooking utensils and groceries at Cirencester, to be independent of lodgings, in case they were not available where needed. To carry the tent and other luggage I intended

*They were his home for the next sixty-eight years.

if possible, to hire a donkey and trap. As it happened these were soon found in a neighbouring village, so I spent the rest of my first day exploring Cirencester, with its magnificent parish church, with a Gothic Town Hall over its porch, sleeping the night at the Fleece Inn, which was comfortable and old-fashioned. Next morning I walked out to the village where the donkey had his quarters, drove him back to Cirencester, picked up my luggage and after lunch we started on our travels. Letting the donkey choose the way, he trotted at a fair pace from Gloucester Street, and then branching off along the Cheltenham Road, proceeded so far as the inn at Perrott's Brook, where he stopped, no doubt assuming that my habits coincided with those of his former master. Here I asserted my preference for a by-road instead of a main highway; we took a lane to the right, slowly climbing a long hill. From the top there was such a charming view of the beautiful little saddle-backed tower of North Cerney church, rising among magnificent trees on the opposite hillside, that I filled the first page of my sketch book, while the donkey nibbled the grass at the roadside. Then, finding that we were at a good place to camp, at the entrance to an old quarry, I pitched my tent and turned Neddy loose in the quarry enclosure, after which I strolled up to a nearby farm to lay in a stock of eggs, butter and milk. After tea I had a most unexpected and, to me, thrilling experience, for taking a look round from the highest part of the ground, I saw silhouetted against the skyline, a man ploughing with two yoke of oxen! There is something so primitive (or should I say classical?) about ploughing with oxen, with their slow stately movements, that this unexpected sight seemed at first as though I were dreaming. For a moment I had a feeling that it was a vision from the time of Virgil and half-forgotten lines from the Eclogues

2

came crowding into my mind. In all those parts of England that I was familiar with, horses had taken the place of oxen long before and I had supposed that the change had been made all over the country, but in Gloucestershire, as I found afterwards, many old customs and ways of life that had long been given up elsewhere, still lingered on and were to do so for nearly another decade. When I asked the farmer about it, he admitted that it was an uncommon sight to see oxen ploughing in these days, but said that he himself had always used them, preferring them to horses. They were slow-moving, but their smaller feet did less harm to the plough-land than horse's hoofs. Later on I found that Lord Bathurst used draught oxen at his home farm in Cirencester Park, and that a farmer at Williamstrip kept a flock of the old white-faced Cotswold sheep, of the breed that had made Cotswold wool famous all over Europe in the middle ages,

though nowadays the heavier fleeces of this breed do not compensate for the coarse mutton.

Next day things did not go so smoothly. To begin with there was trouble with the donkey. When my brother and sisters were small children we had a donkey and trap in which our governess used to drive us out of Norwich into the unspoilt country, which then came quite close up to it. Later, after the donkey had died —much to our mystification, as we had been told you never see a dead donkey—we had a plump white pony named Diamond. Both these animals were normally harnessed by our groom-gardener, but we generally helped him and I flattered myself that I had not forgotten such a simple matter. But I had forgotten the width of a donkey's head, so when I tried to get the collar on in the same way as with a pony, of course it couldn't be done. Naturally, Neddy disapproved of my clumsiness, and after the second attempt was inclined to turn round and shew his heels. Fortunately, just as I was wondering what to do next, a quarryman came up on his way to work, shewed me the easy way to deal with the collar by unbuckling it, and helped me to harness the now by no means patient ass, who very naturally had decided that I had turned the simple operation of harnessing into an uncomfortable performance, which he intended to resist as strongly as he could in the future. However, once the harnessing difficulty had been got over, we started off well enough, along an old Roman road called the Whiteway, in the direction of the famous Roman villa at Chedworth, and the other one at Withington, though I did not visit either of these at the time. We stopped for a few minutes while I made a sketch of the village cross at Calmsden, then, dropping down through a wood, we came to a clearing with a rippling stream running through a green meadow dotted with sheep. The far

side of the meadow was bounded by a low stone wall
flanked by graceful stone piers with moulded caps
bearing richly carved vases. An avenue of ancient
yews and vestiges of terraces and lawns remained to
indicate once stately gardens; while beyond was a
house of the gracious but unpretentious refinement that
characterises the architecture of the time of Charles II.
One wing had evidently been pulled down at some time
and the rest of the house was in a neglected state, badly
in need of repair, but even so the perfect proportions
of the house, with its regularly spaced stone-mullioned
windows and stone-tiled roof, the mellow stone of its
walls contrasting with the dark yews, combined to form
an impression of such haunting beauty that it remains
with me still. I was entranced with the place and
wanted to spend several days making careful drawings
of the house and gardens, but greatly to my disappointment the farmer who lived in the one wing that was
still inhabited, informed me that the property belonged
to a certain peer, who had given strict instructions that
neither camping nor sketching was to be allowed,
"And," said he, "his lordship is a very funny man!"
However, he assured me that his friend, farmer Organ,
in the next village, would let me camp and would also

accommodate the donkey. So with much regret on my part we moved on to the next village, where, I am bound to say, I found farmer Organ as kind and helpful as his friend had said he would be, but the village was only remarkable for some exceptionally grotesque gargoyles on the church tower and for a stone dragon's head spouting water into a large stone trough, which was the village water supply. But before leaving Cassey Compton, as the house was called, I should like to mention a curious thing, though it may be merely a coincidence, in connection with the name. I have at different times seen three other houses either built by the Compton family, or bearing their name, and all three of them have created a deep, if sometimes a melancholy, impression on me. One of them was Kirby Hall in Northamptonshire, now only a magnificent ruin; another was Compton Beauchamp, near the White Horse Hill in Berkshire, a pleasant Elizabethan house, to which has been added a beautifully proportioned stone front of a period not many years later than Cassey Compton. This front is approached from the forecourt by a graceful bridge over a formalised moat. The other house is, of course, Compton Wynyates, which could hardly fail to impress anyone and is so well-known that it needs no description.

My next camping ground was in a green valley at Eyford, about two miles from Stow-on-the-Wold. From here a lane led to Upper Slaughter, Lower Slaughter was a mile beyond, and Bourton-on-the-Water some two miles further on. Upper Swell was also quite near, and as all these villages provided many subjects for my sketch book, I decided to stay there for several days. I actually stayed there between three and four weeks, including a short visit to Campden.

The little rivers of the Cotswolds amply make up for their smallness by their beauty and variety. Clear and swift in their upper reaches, they ripple over their stony beds, forming miniature waterfalls when they encounter larger rocks, with here and there a deeper pool for the trout to hide in. On a convenient rock in the shallows you may see the dipper curtseying to the reflection of his white waistcoat in the water, or along the bankside the blue flash of the kingfisher. Lower down the streams become more placid, meandering through the narrow green meadows at the bottom of the wooded valleys and where they flow through villages crossed by little bridges of an infinite variety of design. Their names, Churn, Coln, Leach, Frome, Windrush and Evenlode, seem to have been happily chosen too. Bibury, Eastleach, Bourton-on-the-Water, and many other riverside villages, gain immeasurably from the combination of their grey stone buildings and the clear sparkling trout streams flowing through them.

Upper and Lower Slaughter are graced with one of these streams, a tributary of the Windrush, which it joins near Bourton-on-the-Water only a mile or two away. At Upper Slaughter the stream runs for the most part through green meadows below the main part of the village, but at Lower Slaughter there is a long stretch of it alongside the village street, crossed by many charming little bridges, some arched in stone, some formed of large paving slabs supported by built-up piers, others of oak planks on stone pillars, simply built according to the whim of their makers, but all with the unconscious beauty of sound traditional workmanship. Lower Slaughter too has its ancient water-mill, while in the grounds of the manor house is a six gabled Tudor dovecote with stone-mullioned windows and four centred arched doorways which itself is almost a manor house in miniature. The manor house at Upper Slaughter, at that time a farmhouse though it has since been enlarged out of all recognition, was a

7

typical example of the smaller Cotswold manor house, with a two-storeyed porch and many gables. In the village, Mr. Lutyens, as he then was, was building a group of almshouses, which as a young architect who much admired his work, though with certain reservations, I thought a great piece of luck, and I soon made friends with the foreman-in-charge, with whose help I filled up some gaps in my knowledge of stone construction. By the kindness of the agent for the Eyford estate I was also enabled to visit the famous stone tile quarries and to learn the details of the ancient craft of stone tile making which has been carried on there at any rate since Roman times, though the Romans for some reason preferred to shape their tiles with pointed ends, as can be seen from those remaining at the Chedworth villa.

All the villages within walking distance were full of interest. At Upper Swell there was another Jacobean

8

manor house with a two-storey porch and a fine great
hall on the first floor. Most of the churches retained
many Norman and even Saxon features, spared by the
later mediæval additions and alterations, while great
ranges of farm buildings splendidly built in the local
stone with stone-tiled roofs surrounded every farmhouse, and picturesque cottages abounded. In those
days, before motoring had opened up the country,
Campden was as remote and self-contained a little
town as could be found, and, except on market days,
peace and quiet seemed to have become its permanent
portion. Every other house in the High Street was,
or had been, an inn, so it was not an easy matter to
decide which to choose for a lodging. In the end, after
well-balancing the pros and cons of each, I chose the
Swan from its fine old sign and found I had made an
excellent choice. The bar was pleasantly old-fashioned,
while its frequenters were friendly and good-mannered,
not stricken dumb by the advent of a stranger, as
sometimes used to happen at village inns! The innkeeper and his wife, Mr. and Mrs. Skey, were noted,
as I afterwards found out, for making their guests
comfortable, the bedrooms were unpretentious but
scrupulously clean, while Mrs. Skey was a first-rate
cook. It was there that I first enjoyed backbone pie, a
delicious dish, at any rate as made by Mrs. Skey, but
disconcerting at the first introduction, owing to the
large amount of debris left on one's plate after enjoying it, as very little meat is attached to each segment
of bone! It would be useless to try to find the Swan
to-day. Like many other inns in Campden, it is now
a private house, while its fine sign is in a museum.
Soon after my visit, Mr. and Mrs. Skey moved to a
much larger and more important inn, the Lygon Arms,
where they continued to entertain their many guests
as hospitably as possible, but something of the old

personal atmosphere of the Swan could not be transferred to the larger establishment, and I was not the only one of its past guests to regret its passing. And, for that matter, the passing of so many other homely old-fashioned inns in all parts of the country. The village inn was essentially a place where the men of the locality could meet together on an equal footing, to discuss the things they were most interested in, sport, crops, local politics, and so on, over their pints of beer or cider. There they could play games, such as skittles, draughts and darts and enjoy the comforts of good fellowship in a cosy room, away from their wives and families. As a rule the bar was a low ceilinged cosy room with a brick, tiled or stone floor, the lower parts of the walls panelled or match-boarded, oak grained or painted. There was a wide fireplace with an open grate having hobs on each side of it, and on the high mantel-shelf a pair of brass candlesticks, a few china ornaments such as Toby jugs or Staffordshire figures and a clock, unless there was a hanging clock elsewhere in the room. Sometimes there were a few sporting prints or oil paintings of prize bulls, rams or stallions painted by some unknown travelling artist. Often, too, there was an engraving of the local landowner or a coloured lithograph of Queen Victoria. There were no collections of more or less spurious antiques as so many inns are cluttered up with nowadays. The few old bits of china and brass on the mantelpiece or in a corner cupboard were authentic heirlooms of the innkeeper and his wife, as such adding an interest to the room without turning it into the fourth-rate museum that is now so often the only alternative to the modernised bar parlour with its chromium plate and varnish. Both the sham antique and the aggressively modern bar are equally lacking in the atmosphere of cosy hospitality that one found so often in the old country inns, many of which had remained practically unaltered for at least a century and still advertised "livery and bait"—that is, stabling and food for their guests' horses—while, as at that time every farmer had his horse and trap, commercial travellers their cobs and smart gigs, and humbler folk had their pony or donkey and trap, the stabling was in good request.

In the market towns the larger inns catered for the farmers on market days. At these "farmers' ordinaries" the helpings were so lavish that you needed a tremendous appetite to do justice to the prime sirloin or saddle of mutton and vegetables followed by a suet pudding or apple pie and with cheese and celery to finish!

A number of artists and craftsmen had already settled in Campden, including the enthusiastic band of craftsmen under C. R. Ashbee, known as the Guild of Handicrafts, but in this short visit I did not come across any of them, though a few years later I got to know many of them personally. Ashbee himself left Campden soon after, but a few of the original members of the Guild still remain, including George Hart, the deservedly well-known silversmith, and his brother the wood-carver. I made a few sketches at Campden mentally registering a vow to return there for a longer visit at some future date. Stow-on-the-Wold, "where the Devil caught cold," as the local saying claims, I also left for a more leisurely appreciation later. The horse fairs held at Stow in Spring and Autumn are still worth going to see. All kinds of horses, from the great shire horses, hunters, piebald gypsy half-breeds, trained riding ponies and untrained Welsh or Forest ponies, can be seen there with their owners and prospective buyers, including a numerous contingent of gypsies. Of late years the demand for farm-horses has greatly fallen off, but there is still a brisk demand

11

for hunters and children's ponies, so one hopes the fair will survive.

I deeply regretted having to leave this delightful corner of Gloucestershire with its lovely unspoilt villages and forgotten slumbering little towns, many of them taking their very names from local features of the landscape as Stow-on-the-Wold, Bourton-on-the-Water, Aston and Weston-Sub-Edge, and others a little further afield, such as Moreton-in-the-Marsh, Shipston-on-Stour and Shipton and Milton-under-Wychwood, names breathing the spirit of loving pride in, and appreciation for, their own countryside.

I lingered as long as I could, spending nearly a month in the North Cotswolds, after which the day came when I had to leave, so one morning I caught and harnessed the donkey, with the help of the kindly young farmer, Powell by name, whose father had moved to Eyford from Wales not many years before, and started on my way back. I now wanted to get back to Cirencester as soon as possible, as I had been strongly recommended to visit Sapperton and see Ernest Gimson's workshops at Daneway House. I therefore drove straight to Bourton-on-the-Water, where I came to the Fosse Way, the ancient Roman road which would take me direct to Cirencester. Like many other Roman roads the Fosse Way is very straight, but the Romans made no attempt to avoid the hills. From Bourton-on-the-Water to Northleach it is all hills, and not far beyond Northleach Fosse Bridge Hill is a really big one. The donkey didn't take at all kindly to the Fosse Way in consequence, especially after a month's rest, and I had to lead and sometimes almost drag it up the steeper ones. However, we got to Northleach, where I found a stable for him at the Wheatsheaf, leaving me with several very enjoyable hours to spend in and around the noble

12

church with its splendid porch and series of fine brasses. The Wheatsheaf provided me with a good meal and pleasant companions for the evening, one of whom could play accompaniments on the piano for songs and choruses in which all the company joined. Next day there was the Fosse Bridge Hill to climb, but once this formidable obstacle was behind us, the rest of the way was comparatively easy going, so we arrived at Cirencester early enough in the afternoon for me to be able to return the donkey and trap to their owner and get back to the town before tea-time. Next day I walked over to Sapperton, entering Oakley Park at the gates at the top of Cicely Hill, and except for a slight detour at a tree-filled hollow, keeping to the main avenue the whole five miles, only stopping to admire the ten rides, where ten grass-covered ways meet in a great circular patch of grass. Looking back from here towards Cirencester the tower of the parish church was at the end of the vista, while another church, which I afterwards found to be Coates, could be seen at the end of another ride. There are other interesting features in this extensive park. Pope's Seat, a stone arbour in which the poet wrote some of his best-known work while staying with the first Earl Bathurst, who was his friend and patron; King Alfred's Hall, a sham ruin largely built of stone from the demolished Sapperton manor house and near it the Wood House; a charming cottage that would have delighted Kate Greenaway, where lived the head-keeper and his wife, Mr. and Mrs. Neil, who provided delicious teas on the lawns around the cottage, while white peacocks strutted round disdainfully. In another part of the park was the polo ground, while the deer park enclosure was nearer Cirencester, as were the kennels of the famous V.W.H. hounds. These I was to see later, but this time I preferred to get to Sapperton as early as possible, so I

13

did not linger in the park, in spite of all its attractions. Coming at length to the Sapperton Park gates I soon found my way to the village, and after a first look at the church, continued my way along the fine sweeping curve of the village street to the top of Daneway Hill. From halfway down the hill I could see Daneway House across the meadows, and in a few more minutes I had entered the gate and was admiring the beautiful old house. Here Peter Waals, the foreman cabinet-maker, found me, took me over the principal rooms of the house, used then as shew rooms for the furniture, after which he took me round the workshops, and then recommending me to call on Gimson himself, shewed me a footpath across the fields, passing the mouth of the canal tunnel and climbing the hill to Sapperton, near the church. Such furniture as Gimson's I had never seen before, which was no wonder, for although it was traditional to the extent of the use of the best craftsmanship in construction and finish, it was entirely original in design and had an assured distinction which only a master mind could have evolved. In its design, grace of form was combined with extreme simplicity to emphasise the beauty of the wood. Oak, mahogany, burr-elm and ebony were used in different pieces, each of which had its special treatment to bring out the full beauty of the material, while instead of hiding the construction, the perfectly made dove-tails were allowed to make a natural pattern where they occurred. It was a completely new style, but one that had nothing tentative about it. Indeed, it had the assured mastery which only genius could have achieved. The rooms in which it was set out were also very different from what I had expected, with an unusual simplicity and severity of style in the large open fireplaces, while the modelled plaster ceilings had an unusual beauty very local in character. I could have spent several hours most

14

enjoyably studying and admiring the house itself. At the same time no more perfect background could have been found for these superb pieces of furniture than these austerely beautiful rooms.

It had been a wonderful morning, providing me with much to think about as I ate my lunch of bread and cheese at the Bell Inn and afterwards as I rested under a tree on the way to Gimson's cottage. Up to this time my life as a young man training to be an architect had followed fairly normal lines. My three years' apprenticeship being now ended, the usual course would have been to have gained further experience in the office of some well-known London architect for another three or four years, first as an "improver", or unpaid assistant, afterwards for a small salary, in my spare time working at drawings for competitions and attending advanced classes. But such a prospect had no attractions for me. The professional side of

THE BELL INN at SAPPERTON by the author

15

architecture had never appealed to me. I was aware that it was generally considered to be impossible to become a successful architect without living in a town, spending much of one's time making social contacts while most of the actual work was done by one's office staff, but for me it was architecture I was interested in, not making a large income as an architect. My own buildings I wanted to have the basic qualities of the best old houses of their locality, built in the local traditional way in the local materials, but not copying the details which properly belonged to the period in which they were built. By working on these lines I hoped that my buildings would at least have good manners and be able to take their natural place in their surroundings without offence.

Above all I wanted to live in the country, and to live and work in such a place as Sapperton, as Gimson and the Barnsleys were doing, seemed to me the most desirable thing in the world. These considerations and many more I pondered as I lay in the shade of the tree, waiting till it seemed a more reasonable time to introduce myself to Gimson. At last, summoning up my courage, for I was painfully shy of meeting the great man, I made my way along the few hundred yards to his cottage.

He was in his garden talking to his gardener as I came along the drive, but saw me and came as far as his garden gate to meet me. He was a tall, well-built man with a slight stoop, a large rather heavy face, except when he smiled, a brown moustache and wide-open contemplative eyes. His expression was that of a man entirely at peace with himself and all the world. His tweed suit hung loosely on him over a soft shirt and collar, with a silk tie threaded through a ring. Being summer he wore a panama hat instead of his usual cloth cap, but in all seasons he wore heavy hob-

nailed boots, made for him by a cobbler at Chalford.

Welcoming me with the friendliest smile, he led me into his long sitting-room entirely furnished with simple plain oak and ash furniture of his own design. Explaining that I was on a sketching tour, how much I had admired Daneway House and his work that I had seen there that morning, I also mentioned acquaintances of his that I had met in London, feeling all the time how slender were my excuses for breaking in on his privacy. However, he put me at my ease at once by his kindly interest in my explorations in the Cotswolds, asking to see my sketchbook, discussing its contents and laughing heartily over my difficulties with the donkey. Very soon we were talking of my ideas of architecture, aims and ideals and plans for the future, in such a natural and friendly way that I forgot my shyness for good and all as far as he was concerned. Before we parted he had suggested that

I should come to Sapperton for a month on trial, to work with him as an "improver", as soon as I could settle my affairs in London, an offer which I jumped at at once.

Walking back I felt that it had been the most wonderful and delightful day of my life. A dear old couple at Daglingworth gave me an excellent tea in their garden, after which I was soon in Cirencester, which I looked at with new interest, as it was so soon to be my nearest town and shopping centre. Next day I was back again in London, which also wore a different aspect, now that I was leaving it, perhaps for good apart from occasional visits. Three weeks later I said my good-byes and travelled back to begin my new life in Gloucestershire.

Before continuing the narrative of my own life in the Cotswolds, I must explain that I had known Gimson by repute for some years before this. My principal had worked in the same office with him under J. D. Sedding, the church architect, and had a great admiration for him. Owing to his dislike of publicity, material to form an opinion on his architectural work was very scarce, but the few photographs of his cottages in Leicestershire which I had seen had convinced me of his superiority to all other living architects whose work I knew. Of Ernest and Sidney Barnsley I had only heard that they were friends of his, inspired by the same ideals.

To most people even the names of Gimson and the Barnsleys are unknown to-day. Their work still remains inadequately illustrated and described. That all the best modern furniture owes a great debt to them is recognised by its designers. In this respect Gimson's name is secure, if only among craftsmen. But there are still some who consider that the present movement to eliminate all individuality and to bring

18

about a mechanised slave state, call it Communism, Socialism, or "Democracy", as you will, tends to the mass-production, not of happiness but of despair. The teaching of William Morris and Lethaby and the example of Gimson and the Barnsleys has not been entirely in vain, and though it seems that the tide of mechanisation cannot be stemmed, at any rate yet awhile, at least more and more people regret it. It is for these and for those who know something of Gimson and the Barnsley's work, but little or nothing else about them that I have tried in the next chapter to give a sketch of the lives of these three men from the time they went up to London to complete their training as architects. Of their lives before this I can only give a few bald statements.

Ernest Gimson was born in Leicester, his father being Josiah Gimson, who founded the important engineering firm of Gimson & Co. Josiah Gimson was a Secularist, and at the Sunday meetings of the Leicester Secularist Society, lectures were given on Art, Philosophy, and other subjects, often by well-known people, two of whom were William Morris and Oscar Wilde. Morris gave his lecture in 1884, and Gimson, then aged 19, was introduced to him after it, when Morris advised him to go into Sedding's office, when he had completed his articles with the Leicester architect to whom he was apprenticed. From this time onwards Morris was a profound influence in his life. Ernest and Sidney Barnsley were two of the younger sons of one of the partners in John Barnsley & Sons, the builders of Birmingham Town Hall. They, too, may have heard William Morris lecture at Birmingham.

Chapter II

GIMSON AND THE BARNSLEYS

ERNEST GIMSON and Ernest and Sidney Barnsley had met in London, where the first two had been together as assistants to J. D. Sedding, the well-known church architect and friend of William Morris, their lifelong friend Alfred Powell coming into the same office a year later, while Sidney Barnsley was articled to Norman Shaw at the time when Lethaby was his chief assistant. They all soon joined the "Anti Scrape", by which name the Society for the Protection of Ancient Buildings was familiarly known, Gimson being an early member of its committee. At the meetings he saw Morris and Webb, and they were followed by a meal at Gatti's at which generally Morris and Webb were present with several of the younger members, including Lethaby, Gimson, S. C. (now Sir Sidney) Cockerell and Detmar Blow.

For their last two or three years in London, Gimson and Sidney Barnsley shared a floor at 3 Raymond Buildings, Philip Webb being at No. 1 and Lethaby close by in Grays Inn Square. The Arts and Crafts movement, then in its infancy, claimed much of their time and enthusiasm. Lethaby says: "I forget whether Gimson shewed anything at the first exhibition of the Arts and Crafts Exhibition Society held in 1888, but at that held in 1890 he exhibited some admirable pieces of furniture." To design furniture was one thing. To get it made to the standard he required in material and workmanship another, so the next step was for Gimson and Sidney Barnsley to join several other architects to found the firm of Kenton & Co., with the object of making furniture and other craft works to the design of the various partners, carried out with the best possible workmanship and materials. The firm came to an end after two years, but a good deal of experience had been gained, while as each partner had only invested £100 in the business and the remaining stock was divided up between them, each getting four or five pieces, the adventure was not disastrous even from a financial point of view. Meanwhile Ernest Barnsley had married, built himself a house at Four Oaks, near Birmingham, and started practice as an architect. The other two friends did not settle down so soon. Gimson made long tours over a great part of England, measuring and sketching such buildings as appealed to him, followed by a long visit to Italy for the same purpose; while Sidney Barnsley, with his friend R. W. Schultz (now Schultz-Weir), spent several months in Greece, where they made careful and complete drawings of the great Byzantine church at Daphne, afterwards published by Mr. Freshfield, who later commissioned Sidney to build a church. Gimson also built two houses at Leicester and learnt the crafts of modelled plasterwork and the making of rush-seated ladder-back chairs during this time. To these two, architecture and the crafts were so interdependent that they could not settle down to an ordinary architectural practice in a town. In the unspoilt country where tradition in the building and other surviving crafts, such as wheelwright's work and blacksmithing still held good, they felt they could find the right setting for a real revival of building and the handicrafts, free from the taint of commercialism, or the deadly monotony of machine production. So they came to Gloucestershire —all three of them, for Ernest Barnsley, having had little encouragement in Birmingham and disliking the place more and more, sold his house and joined them at Ewen, where they took a small place for a year, as a centre from which to look round for a permanent home.

21

At Pinbury Park they found what promised to be the ideal place for their purpose. A medium-sized house of the seventeenth century, with ample barns and outbuildings, magnificently situated overlooking a deep wooded valley, the house was almost a mile beyond Sapperton village. It had been the home of Sir

PINBURY PARK by F. L. GRIGGS

Robert Atkins, author of *The Ancient and Present State of Gloucestershire*, but had since become a farmhouse, part of Lord Bathurst's estate. The house was in a bad state of repair, while the terraced gardens were jungles of every kind of weed and their walls dilapidated. But apart from neglect, it was a noble relic of better days. At the back of the house was a circle of great wych elms, while to the west was the Nun's Walk, an avenue of enormous yews dating back to the middle ages, when Pinbury was a nunnery, long before the present house was built. Down this avenue the ghost of the nun-housekeeper was said to roll Double Gloucester cheeses! The old farm servant who shewed them round insisted on taking them down into the cellar, full of great barrels of cider. When asked what such a great quantity was used for she laughed and said, "Bless you, Sir, we needs it; my master's son Tom do drink a gallon of cider every night, as sure as God's in Gloucestershire." Later they were able to make as much as 2,000 gallons of cider from one year's crop of apples, which they sold to the neighbouring farmers. The tenant farmer had just died and the property was to let, so they found it was possible to take the house on a repairing lease at a low rent, the land being let to adjoining farmers. They stayed on at Ewen while the first repairs were made to the house and then moved in, Ernest Barnsley, his wife and family into the house, the others into cottages adapted out of the outbuildings. A new cottage was built for a gardener, while the buildings and gardens were gradually repaired and got into order. In the outbuildings there was still ample space for workshops, so here Gimson turned his rush-seated chairs, using a primitive pole lathe, while Sidney Barnsley made simple oak and walnut furniture. After a while a few cabinet-makers were brought in from London to make

The Gimsons and Barnsleys at Pinbury

Left to right: Sidney Barnsley, Miss L. Morley, Ernest Gimson, Mrs E. Barnsley, Mary, Ernest Barnsley, Ethel.

furniture to Gimson's and Ernest Barnsley's designs. At the same time Gimson was building four cottages in the Charnwood Forest, which shewed such a mastery of building in local materials that he at once established a position as an architect without a rival in that particular sphere.

Six years after they had moved in, the new yew hedges had taken shape, lawns and flower borders were in perfect order and the house and buildings were in good repair and had the aspect once again of a fine old country house in a setting of great beauty. No one could have appreciated the charm of the place more than they did, but in the meantime, circumstances had arisen which had not been anticipated when they took the house, for during these four years both Gimson and Sidney Barnsley had married, and their cottages, amply large enough for bachelors, seemed rather cramped quarters to their wives. So it was a most fortunate accident that Lord and Lady Bathurst, themselves not long married at the time, called to see the alterations and were so delighted with the house and gardens in their restored condition that they decided that they would like to have the property back in their own hands.

Lord Bathurst offered the three friends most liberal terms for giving up the lease. They were to be allowed to select sites for their houses anywhere they liked on his estate and to build them at his expense, while their joint rents were to be equal to that paid for Pinbury Park. Every architect wants to build his own house, and to be enabled to do so at someone else's expense is an opportunity given to few! The sites were soon decided on. Ernest Barnsley found a pair of old cottages at Sapperton which were no longer habitable, repaired and altered them, making additions at each end. His charmingly laid out garden extended almost

25

to the site of the old manor house, demolished in the 18th century, and included two great walnut trees that must have been well-grown trees at that time. Gimson chose a site about a quarter of a mile higher up the valley, by a group of splendid beech trees. There he built his delightful thatched cottage and laid out his equally attractive garden. Sidney Barnsley built his house and workshop about midway between the two others.

They were now settled at Sapperton for the rest of their lives and their various activities soon became crystallised. Ernest Barnsley very soon relinquished

his interest in furniture-making, devoting his whole time to architecture; Sidney had his own workshop and, professing to be more interested in making than designing furniture, spent his time alone, producing with loving care as fine pieces of craftsmanship as could be made within the limits he set himself. Gimson, with his far more active mind and wider interests, could never be contented with the limited amount of work he could produce with his own hands. Except for modelled plaster-work, which he continued to carry out himself, with occasional help from Mrs. Gimson and later from me, his time was taken up in making designs for his cabinet-makers and blacksmiths and in supervising their work. When architectural work came to him he still found time to make the drawings and look after the building, but much to his regret, once he became well-known by his furniture, very few clients came to him for building work. It is an unfortunate fact that most people seem to think that it is impossible for anyone to excel in more than one art, despite the many examples to the contrary. In Gimson's case he not only excelled in architecture, furniture designing, metalwork, and modelled plaster, but made some excellent designs for bookbindings, needlework and bookplates. In none of these had any adjustments to be made by the executants in order to make them work. He mastered the possibilities of each craft so that his drawings shewed exactly how his designs could be carried out without the least adjustment.

When he moved to Sapperton he gave up making chairs himself, teaching a pupil to make them instead. There was a small sawmill at Daneway, at the bottom of the valley below Sapperton, and Edward Gardiner, one of the sons of the proprietor, was interested in the chair-making, soon becoming an expert in it. Though the sawmill has long been given up, I am glad to say the chair-making is still carried on near Rugby. For the cabinet-making, workshops were adapted from the old farm buildings at Daneway House, one of the most beautiful and characteristic of the old Cotswold houses, which had then recently been bought by Lord Bathurst. Like Pinbury it had fallen into decay, but it was carefully repaired under Ernest Barnsley's direction, after which it was let to Gimson for use as shew rooms for his furniture, a gamekeeper with his wife and family living in the kitchen wing, acting as caretakers.

Daneway House had been a manor house since the fourteenth century, the great hall and much of the kitchen wing of that period still remaining. Originally the hall had had a central fire, one of the louvres in the roof for the smoke to escape from still remaining, as do the smoke-blackened roof timbers, but in the fifteenth century another fireplace was built, while the room was ceiled with moulded oak beams and joists. In the seventeenth century a tall tower-like wing was added, entered by a short flight of steps from the hall, but with a separate outside entrance from a small courtyard. This portion of the house consists of a sitting-room, with two other rooms over, reached by a turret staircase. Below the sitting-room is a basement entered from the courtyard. All these rooms have their original open stone fireplaces, oak doors and fittings, stone-mullioned windows with diamond paned leaded lights and modelled plaster ceilings. Both walls and the stonework of fireplaces were whitened, making a perfect background for the furniture shewn there.

Gimson never employed a large number of cabinet-makers. He started with four good craftsmen from London; Peter Waals, the Dutch foreman, Davol, Smith and Burchett, all of whom stayed with him to the end. In addition to these, local lads were apprenticed to the work, many of whom became fine craftsmen, while he

Walnut and ebony side–board designed by Ernest Gimson and made by Percy Burchett, Ernest Smith & Peter Waals.

453 hours and 47 hours super–vision by Waals. Brass latches by Alfred Bucknell 55 hours
Handles 48 hrs.

Photograph and details courtesy of Cheltenham Art Gallery and Museums

29

had occasional pupils, but I doubt if there were ever as many as a dozen at any one time in the Daneway workshops. Waals' standard of workmanship was so high that the execution and finish of every piece of furniture had to be as near perfect as it was possible to make it. For the more expensive and elaborately finished pieces this was in every way in accord with Gimson's wishes, but for the plain oak furniture, intended for cottage use, he would have preferred a less exacting standard of finish, both so that it could be produced at a lower cost and also as being more natural for that kind of furniture. He would have liked a finish more akin to that of the village wheelwrights, who worked more by eye and less by measurement than highly-trained cabinet-makers. However, unfortunately, there was much less demand for the plain oak so that he was obliged more and more to rely on the more expensive type of work in order to keep the men employed. Had there been more demand for the simpler work he would probably have got over the difficulty by having a separate workshop and training men for this type of work only. It was a real disappointment that he could not produce this cottage-type of furniture at a price that working class people could afford to pay, but with these highly trained men and the perfect finish required, too many hours were spent on each piece for this to be possible. He had always intended that the maximum price for an oak chest of drawers should be £5 when it was to the simplest possible design, but in this he never succeeded.

Besides the cabinet-makers, Edward Gardiner making chairs at the Daneway sawmills also had one or two apprentices. Up in the village there were two blacksmiths' shops where at times four or five smiths worked. He started with one young man, Alfred Bucknell, who had learnt the craft from his father, a

30

small wheelwright. Starting him on strap hinges, latches and casements for his own cottage, Gimson gradually got him to produce more delicate work in polished steel, brass and copper, as well as wrought iron gates and all kinds of iron work for buildings. Then youths were apprenticed to him, some of them becoming very highly skilled in one branch or another of the work, though Alfred Bucknell always remained the best of them all. Gimson generally started the morning in his drawing office. Then he dropped in

A rush seated chair by Gimson in the author's Oakridge cottage

for a short chat with Sidney at his workshop, after which he went on to the blacksmiths' shops. Most afternoons were spent in his drawing office, but he walked across to Daneway two or three times a week. Work in the drawing office was varied by afternoons in the open shed below when there was modelled plasterwork to be done. This was inevitably a messy job, and I remember a chimney sweep remarking with a grin, "Well, Sir, we're both of us dirty, only mine's black dirt and your's is white." Tea was at 4 o'clock and after tea, if the weather permitted, he always went for a long walk, generally with me, Corin his old bob-tailed sheepdog trailing behind. He was a tremendous walker and had once walked forty miles in a day with his long easy stride. At first I had difficulty in keeping up with him, but after I had developed an equal pace as a natural walking speed my friends complained that they could not keep up with me! On these walks we had the most delightful discussions on almost every subject, while he was perpetually on the look-out for signs and sounds of the wild life around him. He knew most bird calls, the haunts of badgers and foxes, where the dipper nested and the red squirrel had his drey. A fine tree he admired as much as a fine build-ing. Anecdotes of William Morris and Philip Webb, both of whom he had known in his London days, were interspersed with discussions on philosophy, folk-lore, the revival of the crafts, and almost every subject except politics and religion. His gospel was that of William Morris, of healthy employment for all in making useful and beautiful things or productive agri-culture, giving everyone an intelligent interest in their work, time to do it as well as might be, with reasonable leisure for other interests. In his Utopia the greater part of the population would live in villages, each largely self-supporting with their farms, mills, wheelwrights, carpenters, masons and other tradesmen. There would be small towns producing goods beyond the capacity of the villages, and forms of culture and entertainment for their immediate districts, while a few larger towns would be centres of government, research, specialisation, and so on. He was well aware that the Socialists of the time were as much opposed to the conception of happiness in and by work as the industrialists, but he hoped that by making a small beginning the movement would gain adherents and ultimately become a force to be recognised. He planned to found a craft village on these lines and had got so far as to buy the land and make sure of a water supply for it about two miles from Sapperton. Then the 1914-18 war prevented any further progress and he died so soon after that the whole project came to nothing. He hated mechanisation in any form and would allow no machinery of any sort in his workshops, not even a circular saw. For the same reason he was proud of the fact that there was nothing made by machinery in his house except the plumbing, which was a concession to his wife! For him a log fire on the open hearth provided more comfort to the eye as well as the body than the stuffy heat of radiators. In religion he was an agnostic and preferred not to discuss religion with anybody, as being a matter that everyone should decide for himself. Believing that example is better than precept he thought that the aim of everyone should be to add to the store of happiness and beauty in the world instead of wasting time on religious forms and ceremonies. Tolerant of other people's ways of life, his own personal habits were carefully regulated, and not without a certain austerity. He preferred a rush-seated chair to an upholstered one, plain lime-washed walls to wallpapered, plain home-made food to imported luxuries. He was not a teetotaler but was almost a total abstainer. With all this he enjoyed a good joke as well as anyone, even if it was against himself, as when a London cabby, seeing him standing at a corner hesitating to cross the street and wearing his heavy hobnailed boots, called out to him, "Hallo, guv'nor, how are the crops?" He loved all simple fun, good music and country dancing, and was one of the first to appreciate Arnold Dolmetsch for the one and Cecil Sharp for his work in reviving the other. Dolmetsch stayed at Pinbury, while Cecil Sharp made several visits to Sapperton, which under his and his wife's guidance was one of the first villages to take up the old dances again. He had a good baritone voice and enjoyed singing such songs as "Turmut Hoeing", "The Leather Bottel" and a curious old local song called "Tom Ridler's Oven" as well as many from Gilbert and Sullivan's operas. The old folk songs and country dances with their delightful airs, then only just re-discovered, especially delighted him, and every Saturday evening he joined the class of boys and girls at the village hall, learning the new dances as they came out, while Mrs. Gimson played the piano. It pleased him when he found out that several of the dances had been popular in the neighbourhood within living memory, the postman remembering dancing some of them at Harvest Homes in his boyhood. This postman also knew the old Mummer's Play and brought the mummers round every Christmas. In various villages not many miles away, as at Bampton and Headington in Oxfordshire, Morris and Sword dances as well as country dances still survived, encouraging him to feel that it was not too late to revive this healthy and enjoyable form of relaxation in Sapperton.

Nowadays, after two world wars and the uneasy period between them, Gimson's hope for a society based on the simple life and the substitution of hand work for machinery must appear as the dream of a visionary, but up to 1914 it did not seem so impossible, although conditions had steadily moved in the direction of the machine age since William Morris first advocated that way of life. Before 1914, however, country districts were little affected, mechanisation being almost entirely confined to the towns. In the Cotswolds masons, carpenters and stone-tilers had all the traditional skill and pride in their work as their forefathers. The same could be said of the wheelwrights, blacksmiths, saddlers and other country craftsmen. Agricultural workers, too, were more highly skilled, perhaps from having started work so much earlier in their lives, while most of them had other crafts at their fingers' ends and could build a shed or a dry wall. Motor cars were still only rich men's toys and the only regular communication with the towns was by the weekly carrier's cart. In building, only horse-drawn transport being available, it was still the natural and cheapest way to use local materials. The stone came from the village quarry or was dug on the site; stone tiles for the roofs were quarried less than five miles away and oak and larch for the timbers could be had from the estate.

After the 1914–18 war it was soon found that these simple ways had gone for ever. Many of the older and most highly skilled craftsmen had died or retired, while the younger men returned from the war had no sympathy with the old ways. Much of the traditional skill in building was gone, while with the coming of the motor lorry brickwork became cheaper than stone, and all kinds of manufactured materials were much more easily obtained. So it became more and more difficult and expensive to build in the old way, new cottages were built of brick and roofed with concrete tiles, barns were re-roofed with corrugated iron and there were many other innovations, until it soon became rare to find a village still entirely built of local materials. It was the same story with other village crafts. The wheelwrights still carried on for a few more years in a much reduced way, chiefly making gates and fences and repairing carts, but they made no new wagons. They could not compete in price with the town wagon works and though there was no comparison between their work and the mass-produced articles for workmanship or convenience in use, the farmers bought the cheapest. However, Gimson did not live to see these conditions. At the end of the war he was already a sick man, though by the irony of fate he was at last getting some important commissions in architecture. Some of these were in association with the late Frederick L. Griggs, R.A., who had become one of his greatest friends, for whose wonderful etchings of the England of the middle ages and the immediate past, both he and I had an almost unbounded admiration. Others came from old clients for furniture. As long as he was able to, he worked at these, as well as at drawings for furniture and metalwork with Griggs' and my help, but he was to see none of them come to fruition. After his death his plans for Bedales School Library were carried out under Sidney Barnsley's supervision, but the other projects were abandoned, most of them owing to the vastly increased cost of building at the time. At Daneway a nucleus of the older men had been kept on all through the war, while several of the younger men returned after it was over. There was plenty of demand for the finest furniture, so the workshops were as busy as they had ever been. It seemed as if at last Gimson's genius was beginning to be fully appreciated, and had he lived for even a few more years he would have left behind him important architectural works which would have won him much more than the limited fame which the few small houses and cottages he actually built had already achieved for him. But this was not to be. He died in August 1919 in his 55th year and was buried in Sapperton churchyard.

Mrs. Gimson, whom he married in 1900, survived him till 1940. She was the daughter of a Yorkshire rector and niece of Archbishop Thompson. She had many good qualities, taking a keen interest in all village activities and helping him in many ways in his work, while she was an excellent housekeeper. But she was the type of person who made no intimate friends and preferred to have little to do with the wives and families of Ernest and Sidney Barnsley, in spite of their friendship with her husband. After his death she continued to interest herself in village activities as well as in numerous committees elsewhere, living alone except for one old servant.

The Daneway workshops were closed soon after Gimson's death, but Peter Waals, the Dutch foreman, started new workshops at Chalford, keeping most of the men on. Here he produced much excellent work until his death in 1938. Edward Gardiner had already left the district, but he continues to make the rush-seated chairs to Gimson's designs at Prior's Marston, near Rugby. Alfred Bucknell, too, still works at Water Lane, about three miles from Sapperton, and as his son now works with him there is hope of some continuity in this branch of craftsmanship.

Of his buildings, the two houses he built at Leicester, the house at Budleigh Salterton, the five cottages in Charnwood Forest and two at Kelmscott still remain. Also the hall and library at Bedales School, but his own cottage at Sapperton was burnt down during the last war. *Leicester Museum and Art Gallery has some of his furniture and metalwork, and there are one or

*There is now a large collection at Cheltenham and a smaller one at Arlington Mill Museum, Bibury, Gloucestershire.

37

two examples in Cheltenham Art Gallery.

For an authoritative description of his work I must quote from Professor Lethaby's chapter in *Ernest Gimson, His Life and Work*, published by the Shakespeare Head Press in 1924. He says: "Gimson's furniture was, it seems to me, one kind of perfect, that is it was useful and right, pleasantly shaped and finished, good enough but not too good for ordinary use. His furniture from the Kenton time and increasingly when he had his own workshops and trusted men, was much more than his 'design'. Every piece was thought definitely for particular picked woods and for clearly understood ways of workmanship and his supervision was so constant and thorough that the design was changed in process of making as the materials and working might suggest."

"His modelled plasterwork was entirely his own handiwork and was at least equally perfect.... The distribution, type of relief and final expression are easy, masterly and just right, quite original and modern, but as good, every bit, as old work, and yet as simple as piecrust. He saw his building work through stone, brick, cob and wood: his direct knowledge of two crafts gave him a sympathetic understanding of all, and always he kept within his strength; his works were not sham grandeurs and vain ambitions of paper promises, but they were buildings."

If, as I have said, there was a certain austerity about Gimson's personal habits, it was never allowed to obtrude itself in any way in his association with other people, but for Sidney Barnsley austerity was almost a religion. He had his cold bath every morning, even in the depth of winter, until, towards the end of his life, when having developed heart trouble as well as lumbago, his doctor insisted on his giving it up. He thought it wrong to delegate dull or unpleasant work to others, and so a great deal of his time was taken up by gardening and sawing and splitting wood for the winter fires. Thorough and methodical in all that he did, he mastered the craft of cabinet-making until he succeeded in making furniture with his own hands as near perfect in workmanship as could be. Its design only just fell short of Gimson's, to which it bore a legitimate resemblance, being based on the same principles and theories. Extremely conscientious as he was, he was also kind and generous, always willing to help anyone who came to him for advice. I admired his work and respected his ideals but found it a little difficult to be entirely in sympathy with them. Rightly or wrongly I felt that he set a standard of life too rigid for ordinary people like myself to attain to, but though this side of him did not appeal to me, he was most kind and hospitable, and I had many enjoyable games

SIDNEY BARNSLEY

of tennis with him on Saturday afternoons, as well as cricket and rounders with him, his, and his brother's children. That he was likeable was proved by his many friends, both among his fellow craftsmen and his clients. His wife had the great misfortune to be stone deaf, but she had learnt to lip-read and was so kind and capable, with a real sense of humour that her personality to a large extent triumphed over this disability. They had two children, Grace and Edward, and it was characteristic of Sidney that, loving his Sapperton home as he did, he took a small house in Cirencester for some years so that they could go to a day school there, himself bicycling to his workshop at Sapperton and back every day. Later they were sent to Bedales School at Petersfield, near which village Edward ultimately settled, following in his father's footsteps in the making of fine furniture, though not like him limiting his output to what he could make with his own hands.

After Gimson's death, Sidney supervised the building of the library at Bedales School, the drawings for which Gimson had completed, and for the remainder of his life he practised as an architect, carrying out several big works of alterations and additions, building the Gyde Almshouses at Painswick, and cottages at Miserden and elsewhere, his architectural work having the quiet distinction that had been such a feature in his furniture. He was the last survivor of the three friends, dying suddenly in 1926 at the age of 61.

There was nothing of the ascetic about Ernest Barnsley. A big, handsome, jolly type of man, fond of good company, good food and good cheer of every sort, he was built on a large scale altogether. He always referred to Sidney as "The boy", though he was actually only two years his senior, and while he was on affectionate terms with him, seemed to take it

ERNEST BARNSLEY & FAMILY

41

for granted that his extra years gave him a permanent superiority. All other people, however much younger than himself, he treated as equals and friends, provided that they shared at least some of his tastes and were willing to accept his hospitality. His architectural work had a fine breadth and simplicity. He always had as much work as he wanted to do in his leisurely way, making all his own drawings and spending a great deal of time supervising the work, often staying with his clients, who enjoyed his company. A real *bon viveur*, he enjoyed not only eating a good dinner but buying the ingredients and cooking it himself, with his wife's and daughters' assistance. Wherever he went he collected recipes for good dishes or the addresses from whence he could obtain special delicacies. His York hams and Wensleydale cheeses came from farms in Yorkshire direct. Welsh mutton from Brecon and pork pies from Melton Mowbray. Cirencester being a market town and agricultural centre had good grocers', fishmongers' and poulterers' shops and one good wine merchant's. So, once or twice a week he would cycle into the town, returning with his bicycle laden with parcels hanging from every possible part of it, riding very slowly, often reading a book open on his handlebars. His sloe gin he made himself and loved to regale his many visitors on it. It was stored in old round-bellied bottles holding up to a gallon, and I well remember his cry of anguish when he once slipped on the stone steps leading down to his cellar and broke one of them, wasting nearly a gallon of the precious liquid. He was also a connoisseur in old furniture, glass and china, taking a great delight in hunting for unusual pieces in antique shops wherever he found them. Some of his clients, many of whom were wealthy, would send him presents of game, salmon or trout, which gave him the excuse for a party, most of the day being spent in preparing for it. His wife, being from Yorkshire, also had some good family recipes. Like him she appreciated good living and was equally hospitable, so all through the summer there were friends or relations staying in the house, while casual visitors to the village were invited to meals and a chat over a glass of sloe gin in his comfortable library if they shewed the least interest in his hobbies or work. One such young man came with a slight introduction from an acquaintance at Broadway. Witty and amusing and a brilliant conversationalist, mentioning many well-known artists and writers as his personal friends, he was invited to tea, dinner and then to stay the night. After staying for three days he happened to mention a friend of his who had been invited to a house for a week-end but had stayed thirteen years! This was too much even for Ernest Barnsley's spacious ideas of hospitality and the young man had to be given a hint to leave next day which he could not mistake, but he had meantime made other acquaintances in neighbouring villages and soon after took a cottage about three miles away with two of the sons of a famous artist to whom he was then tutor. Later it was rumoured that deciding to visit Baghdad he had started across the desert pushing a perambulator full of fancy goods to barter with the Arabs for food, but the 1914-18 war coming on, had been captured and imprisoned by the Turks. Since then nothing has been heard of him at Sapperton.

Ernest Barnsley's most important work was Rodmarton Manor, probably the last house of its size to be built in the old leisurely way, with all its timber from local woods, sawn on the pit and seasoned before use. For Coates Manor he used the materials from Ham House, an Adams mansion near Birmingham which had been scheduled for demolition. He also had important work in Wales, near Wrexham, and built a charming cottage on Dartmoor. He could have had many more important houses to build if he had cared to undertake the work, but preferred to make all his own drawings and do his own supervision, so he seldom had more than two or three jobs on at one time.

RODMARTON MANOR

CHAPTER III

FRAMPTON AND OAKRIDGE

WHEN I started work for Ernest Gimson there was no suitable accommodation at Sapperton for me, but I found comfortable diggings at Frampton Mansell, a hamlet on the same side of the valley about a mile lower down. Here there were a few picturesque cottages, the manor farm, a fine house on a small scale, of the time of Charles II, and a good inn, which was a free house in the hands of a local family which had owned it for several generations. The church, a pseudo-Norman structure, had been built about sixty years previously. There were some exceptionally fine wych elms in and below the village, but no actual woods near to it. The cottage where I lodged looked out across the valley to the scattered village of Oakridge Lynch on the opposite side. In the lane outside there was a series of great stone troughs fed by a spring and this was the water supply. Mrs. Elliot, my landlady, was a taciturn but kindly old lady, who had been a housekeeper, kept the cottage spotless and was a good cook, so I was comfortable enough for the few months I was with her. After that time I found an empty cottage at Oakridge Lynch; a tiny little place with one sitting-room and a long narrow room where a loom for wool-weaving had been fixed, with two bedrooms upstairs. There was a well and a small garden with a few currant and gooseberry bushes. The rent was 1/- a week, which I paid quarterly to my landlady, Mrs. Chapman, who lived at one of a pair of cottages called the Frith, about two miles away, the other cottage being used partly as a pig-sty! Mrs. Chapman had known better days. She was the only daughter of the last miller at Henwood Mill, in Dorvel Wood, opposite Sapperton,

45

VILLAGE SPRING
FRAMPTON MANSELL
GLOS
AUG. 1929.

W.G.S.

and had inherited some property at Oakridge, including the Frith cottages and the one she let to me. Unfortunately she was disfigured by a lupus, a large crimson patch on the side of her face, and being left alone in the world when her parents died, despairing of getting a husband in any other way owing to her misfortune, she advertised for one in the local paper. As a result she married a drunken good-for-nothing named Chapman, who was a terror to the neighbourhood, driving his pony and trap at breakneck speed through the narrow and steep lanes of Oakridge and Tunley, swearing and threatening everyone and everything that got in his way, a habit which frequently landed him in jail, to the temporary relief of the local inhabitants. His father had been a well-to-do man, owning the last of the silk mills at Oakridge. He had had a lot of trouble with this, his eldest son, so when he died he left him an annuity of £100 a year, the rest of his fortune going to his younger son, who, however, spent it all in a few years, but after having had his fling settled down respectably as a rate-collector! The eldest son usually got through his quarterly allowance in a few weeks, during which time he was almost continuously fighting-drunk, so his unfortunate wife had a very poor time of it.

I lived alone in my cottage at Oakridge for about a year, but as I enjoyed being independent and looking after myself, I was never lonely. After an early breakfast I had a walk of about a mile to Water Lane, where Gimson was altering and adding to a fair-sized house, and then on to Sapperton through the small hamlet of Tunley and across the valley by the old pack-horse road through "The Gulf", now only a footpath almost knee-deep in beechleaves as it descends through Dorvel Wood into the valley, but with a milestone half-way down it with a large V cut on it, as being five miles from Cirencester. Till about a century before, this had been the only road from Stroud and Bisley to Cirencester. Tunley Lane was a great place for wild flowers. Periwinkle and the deep crimson Bloody Cranesbill grew there, as well as a pink flowered wood sorrel, so at Gimson's suggestion I picked and brought with me a different wild flower each day and made a drawing of it. This was part of his training of me in design and I soon found how differently one must look at a flower, or any other natural object, for this purpose. At first my drawings were as realistic as I could make them, with the accidental peculiarities of leaf and flower of the sprig I had brought with me, but he soon taught me to note only its special characteristics, making a simplified analysis of the basic peculiarities of the plant and then adapting this to a pattern suitable for modelled plaster, wood-carving or needlework as the case might be. I generally reached Gimson's cottage between ten and eleven, by which time he was back in his drawing office from his daily visit to the blacksmith's shop. The rest of the morning and the afternoon were spent at modelled plasterwork, or architectural details. For the furniture and metal-work he made almost all the drawings himself. While I was living at Oakridge he always gave me lunch and tea, and after tea I could start on my three mile walk back as soon as I was inclined. Back again at my cottage I had my little bit of garden to cultivate, neighbours to chat with, and on winter evenings plenty of books to read. I got to know some of the villagers, many of whom were masons or stone-tilers, glad to tell me of their crafts, or of local events and history. Oakridge folk were very independent. The village had come into being mostly by the action of "squatters" who had built their cottages on the common, it being the custom, if not the law, that if anyone could get so far in building as to have smoke coming from his chimney he could not be dispossessed. So most of them owned their own cottages freehold and were scornful of the inhabitants of Sapperton and Frampton who either rented theirs, or whose cottages would in time pass to their landlords.

The common, a very extensive one, with the adjoining Bisley Common, of which it probably had originally been part, had only been enclosed within living memory, an event causing much bitter feeling at the time. Some of the older men chuckled as they told how on dark nights gangs of men collected in the village and demolished many yards of the dry stone walls, dividing what had been the common, at a time. The chief beneficiary of the enclosure was the then lord of the manor, Sir John Dorrington, who had made himself so unpopular by promoting it that, when he put up for parliament, crowds ran beside his carriage chanting "Who stole the donkey's dinner?" That the villagers resented the loss of their common rights of grazing animals and cutting timber, is easy to understand. All they got in exchange was a small plot of ground each, often some distance from their home, which they were obliged to fence in. This many of them could not afford to do, so they accepted instead of the land a load of firewood at Christmas-time every year for a few years, after which it ceased altogether. Another fairly recent episode was the Pest House affair. There was a serious outbreak of smallpox at Stroud not long after the enclosure of the common, and the Stroud Town Council purchased a house in an isolated position at Oakridge bordering on what had been the common, intending to use it as an isolation hospital. But the Oakridge people objected to having smallpox cases brought to their village, and having protested without effect, took the law into their own hands and burnt the

49

house down. Several of them were prosecuted, but at any rate they got their way; Stroud having to find another site for their isolation hospital. The house was re-built and is now a small farm, but is still called the Pest House.

A very large proportion of the inhabitants at that time were surnamed Gardiner, owing, it was said, to an exceptionally prolific innkeeper of that name who flourished about a century before. Although most of his many children were born out of wedlock, he acknowledged them all as his own, so that they took his name. In consequence, many of the younger men having the same Christian names, it was difficult to distinguish between them in writing or conversation. Fortunately their fathers' Christian names had been mostly chosen in the old-fashioned way, by opening the Bible at random and taking the first name of the right sex that came, so there were Eli, Seth, Caleb and Job Gardiner and several other such biblical names, and the problem of the identity of the next generation was solved by adding the father's name after the son's. So Harry Seth Gardiner was not confused with Harry Caleb, while Albert George Eli Gardiner, though rather a mouthful, identified its owner without any question. What happened about the next generation I have not heard, but there is so much more moving to other localities now than there was at that time, that the difficulty has probably been got over in that way.

While I was living at Oakridge I had occasional visitors. With one of my friends who used to come down for week-ends, I tramped many miles in search of a genuine old recipe for making mead. After many trails had been followed in vain, we found an old house at Edge, near Painswick, romantically placed overlooking the Severn Valley, where we tasted the mead made by the farmer's wife and saw the bees collecting

honey for the next brew. The good lady wrote out
the recipe, adding to it another for metheglin, a lighter
beverage made from the combs. She didn't see many
visitors at the isolated farmhouse so she enjoyed the
opportunity for a chat and willingly told us all she
knew of the secrets of brewing this nectar of drinks.
Later on I made the mead, fermenting it in a large
red earthenware panchion, with yeast spread on toast
floating on the surface, as well as sprigs of rosemary
and other herbs, and after it had finished "working",
bottling it in two-gallon stoneware jars which, following our friend's instructions, were not to be touched
for at least six months. As a special liqueur to offer
visiting friends I found it very useful and it lasted a
long time, improving with age. Some which I re-
bottled in an ancient wine bottle of Elizabethan type,
was put away and forgotten for more than ten years,
after which time it had gained in character more than
it had lost in sweetness. Mead is said to have the
property of making you drunk from the waist down-
wards, but I have never had enough to put this to the
test! About this time I also made some cowslip wine.
I collected three small boys and their sisters and sent
them out picking cowslips. They came back with large
bunches and the next business was to pick off all the
flowers or "pips", as no leaf or stem can be used.
The boys soon tired of this, but their sisters were more
conscientious, sticking to the job well, so that I soon
had enough pips for a brew. I gave them a substantial
tea, an orange and sixpence each, with which they went
home delighted! Cowslip wine is clear and pale golden
in colour, but like most other English home-made wines
is only a poor substitute for the fermented juice of the
grape. I have tasted many of the others, including
sloe, blackcurrant, rhubarb, dandelion and parsnip, but
not plum jerkum, which is made extensively in the

51

North Cotswolds and has a great reputation for potency. While on the subject I may as well mention a pleasant experience in which another kind of home-made wine played a part, although it actually happened a year or two later. One of Gimson's sisters had asked her brother to build her a holiday cottage in the Charnwood Forest. While this was being built he sent me down for a few days to make sure that the builder was carrying out the work in the way he wanted. The Charnwood Forest is a grand tract of primitive woodland country, in which are several dis-used slate quarries which have become picturesque lakes, with steep rocky sides formed of the beautiful many-coloured slate of that district. Being in the middle of the woods, well away from any village these lakes are charming features of the landscape and have also become the haunt of kingfishers and wild fowl of many kinds. The builder took me to one of them to select some slabs of slate for lintels over the doors and windows of the cottage, and I found it so attractive that I should have liked to have greatly prolonged my visit there, but of course I couldn't keep him away from his business. While on this excursion I stayed in a cottage in the forest with an old retired farm-labourer and his wife, a real Darby and Joan couple. On the wall hung a fine array of brightly polished brass horse ornaments, some attached to their martingales. They were old ones handed down from earlier genera-tions, with a new one added now and then, many of them worn with much polishing, but as fine a collection as I have seen. In the evening he drew three glasses of wine out of a small cask and invited me to drink with him and his "missis". It was birch wine, made from the sap of the birch tree, collected in the Spring by boring a hole in the bark and inserting a wooden spout. The sap drips into a bucket left underneath it till it is full. The actual making of the wine is much the same as with most other home-made wines, but the sap takes the place of water and gives it a distinctive flavour and body, resulting in a liquor rather like vermouth. An easily made refreshing summer drink, effervescent with a flavour of muscatels, is elder flower water, or frontiniac, but it has the disadvantage that it generates so much gas that it blows the corks out of the bottles and often even breaks the bottles themselves.

My mother came for a week-end, but I am afraid found the conditions rather too primitive for her liking. Two or three days after she had left I found a pudding she had made for me sometime when I was out, which she had put in a cupboard which I hadn't since opened. By the time I discovered it, the pudding had grown a fine crop of blue mould, so I asked the woman who came daily to wash up and tidy the cottage, to throw it away.

"I wouldn't throw that away, Sir," she said. "I'll take it to my sister-in-law; she's got a lot of young children as'll be glad of it!"

"But surely she wouldn't let them eat it?"

"Why, bless you, Sir, they'll get it into them alright."

And I suppose they did! Another accident I had was in trying to stew some blackcurrants. I left them too long in the pan, so when I took it off the fire I found I had made jam instead!

On Saturday afternoons and Sundays I explored most of the country round within about a ten mile radius, one of my favourite walks being up the Througham Valley. This valley joins the Stroud Valley near the Red Bridge, the first one over the canal below Daneway. It continues up past Tunley to a fine old house called Rookwoods, then winds on through meadows full of the early purple orchis past a farm called Battledown, near which grew wild daffodils, with

Juniper Hill on the opposite side, where the dark wind-blown bushes straggle up the steep hill, looking strangely like a retreating army. Battledown is said to have got its name from a battle between the Danes and Saxons. A little further on is the site of The Greys, once a Jacobean house of some importance, but all that now remains of it are the bases of a pair of great stone piers that once bore the drive gates. Of the house itself nothing remains, though an old man who had been born in a cottage a mile away told me that he had often been there when it was a farmhouse, and said that the floors of some of the rooms were carpeted with tapestries from the walls! The house was demolished by Sir John Dorrington, who used some of the materials, including a fine oak staircase, for an enlargement of his house at Lypiatt Park. About a mile further on was the most attractive house called Througham Slad, and then two more fine houses at Througham. Beyond Througham was Honeycombe Farm, and beyond that, across the head of the valley, Wishanger, a house with a three-storey porch. Nearly all these houses had once been either manor houses or at least the homes of members of such families as the Hancocks of Daneway, or the Smarts of Bisley, but had sunk to the position of farmhouses, most of them rather neglected, but still fine examples of Cotswold buildings of the 16th to the 18th centuries.

A mile or two away was Bisley, a large village that had once been a place of some importance in the middle ages, when it boasted a High Constable. The remains of a market hall can still be seen built into the Bear Inn. There are many old traditions connected with the village, which is still known locally as "Bisley God help us", a name it has borne, it is said, since the fourteenth century when the parish was placed under an interdict owing to a curious accident. According to the tradition, some masons were repairing the stone-work of the holy well, which is still an interesting feature of the churchyard. They were sitting on the coping round the well-head having their midday meal when, just as the church clock struck one, a portion of the stonework gave way and one of them fell backwards into the well and was drowned. There is still a local saying, "There goes one, as Pearce (Piers?) said, when he fell down the well", referring to this very event, the consequences of which were serious, as the well, being holy and on consecrated ground, its pollution, even by an accident, was a sufficient cause for the bishop to place the parish under an interdict. While the interdict was in force no parishioner of Bisley might be buried in the diocese, so the dead had to be taken all the way to Bibury, twelve miles away. This sounds like a tall story, but by way of confirmation the bridge over the Churn at Perrots Brook, which is on what was, up to the nineteenth century, the nearest way from Bisley to Bibury, is still called Bier's Way, and a part of Bibury churchyard is called "Bisley Piece"!

Another story is the legend of the Bisley Boy who became Queen Elizabeth! This tells how the young princess stayed a night at Butler's Court, an old house adjoining the churchyard, where she unfortunately died! Her guardians, fearing the king's wrath, searched the whole parish for another red-headed little girl of the same age in vain and were obliged to substitute a boy for her, who for the rest of his life had to dress and act as first the princess and then the Queen, which accounts for the fact that Queen Elizabeth never married and was such a powerful ruler when she came to the throne! Needless to say, there are no records confirming this legend and there is reason to believe that it was started as a joke by some of the younger members of the Keble family, a brother of the celebrated leader of the Oxford Movement having been the vicar of Bisley responsible for restoring the church. Before this restoration the church must have been a very interesting one, but the work was done so thoroughly that little of the original structure remains except the effigy of a knight under a 14th century canopy, now on the outside wall of the chancel, some brass and bronze tablets commemorating members of some once important local families, and the font with its very primitive representation of the miraculous draught of fishes. Some of the villagers say that this carving was the work of a curate at the time of the restoration of the church, and it may well be, though antiquarians who have seen it have declared it to be early Norman work. Beyond Bisley, at the head of the beautiful Slad valley running down to Stroud, is another fine old farmhouse, with affinities to one of those at Througham two miles away, called Sydenhams, which has an elaborate carved Jacobean bedstead built into an attic. There is a hidden recess in the head of the bed to hold a sword, presumably so that the owner could protect himself and family if the lonely house was attacked at night. A small village called The Camp is about two miles away. Here there are two pre-historic barrows which have been desecrated at some time, shewing the great slabs of stone which had formed the burial chambers. At that time the Camp Inn was a very cosy one, in the bar of which there was a green-painted settle known as "Tom Halliday's Throne", in honour of a well-known local character who could be found seated on it every evening for many years. When the old man grew too rheumaticky to hobble to the inn some of his friends clubbed together and bought the settle, so that he could be enthroned by his own fireside for his remaining years.

Let us hope that his pint mug and the wherewithal to fill it were not forgotten either! At The Camp lived old Jesse Freeman, a master builder who employed a good many men, but it was a mystery to me how he managed his business, as he was never to be found at his builder's yard. When you wanted him you could always find him at Througham Fields, chipping away making stone tiles, in the open if it was a fine day, or in an open-sided shed if it was wet. There he was, as happy as a sandboy, working at the craft he loved and always ready to talk about stone tiles, their different varieties and the right and wrong way of laying them. He must have made millions of them in his time, and was still making them when he was over eighty. Beyond The Camp it was only a few minutes' walk to White-way Colony, a socialist settlement established some twenty years earlier. The settlement consisted of a collection of small wooden shacks with corrugated iron roofs, dotted about promiscuously over the land on both sides of a lane, and was a decided blot on the landscape. The colonists were said to include a number of cranks, including some nudists, but that side of it was probably exaggerated. There was certainly a good weaver there and, I believe, other craftsmen, while I know that there was an excellent baker, who made delicious whole-meal bread from stone-ground English flour, and as I had no facilities for baking my own bread I was glad to get it from the best baker, whatever his ideas on other subjects than baking might be. A different road out of The Camp brought one to Sheepscombe, a picturesque village on the way to Painswick, which is so well-known that I won't attempt to describe it here. There were other walks towards Stroud, either along the towing path, or by Bournes Green, where, at Lilyhorn House, lived the last male survivor of the Hancocks family, or by Lypiatt Park.

As I can't avoid frequent mention of the Hancocks family, I will now say something of their history. Daneway House belonged to the Clifford family in the 14th century, when they obtained permission to have their own private chapel there. During this century it was for a time a dower house, let at a rent of one red rose at midsummer! Was this a memory of Fair Rosamund, a Clifford of an earlier century! It was bought by the Hancox family (the name is spelt either way in old documents), in 1397. It was then a manor house with a considerable estate, including the whole of Tunley, with King's Farm and Hill House, both good-sized houses, and a great deal of woodland over-looking the Sapperton valley. For more than two centuries the family seem to have been content to live quietly as squires and farmers, taking no active part in public affairs, but in the Civil War they took sides with Cromwell, W. Hancox of Daneway being one of Cromwell's captains who was with him when he turned out the Rump Parliament. Cromwell made him High Sheriff of Bisley Hundred, and according to local tradition he built the tall portion of Daneway House as a guest-house for Cromwell when he visited him there. This part of the house has all the characteristics of Jacobean work, but it is quite possible, being in such a remote part of the country, that there was a con-siderable time-lag in the style of building and that the addition may belong to this time. W. Hancox died in 1670 and was buried in Bisley church, where there is a brass tablet to his memory. His descendant, Thomas Hancocks, attended George III when he opened the canal tunnel. He was a man of huge proportions and great strength, weighing twenty stone and, it is said, once picked up a man who offended him and dropped him over the bridge into Daneway Lock. He died in 1792, leaving the Daneway House property to his only daughter, Mrs. Bidmead of Frampton. After her death it was sold to a Chalford stick manufacturer, who cut down a great deal of the woods and re-sold it to a Mr. Chapman, owner of the Oakridge Silk Mill and, incidentally, the father of my landlord. He sold it to a builder, who finally sold it to Lord Bathurst in 1899. A collatoral branch of the family lived at King's Farm at Tunley, a house with an avenue of walnut trees leading to it. A tragedy occurred here in 1832 when the farm was in the occupation of H. W. Hancocks, then aged 23, three men carrying out a plan to rob him of a sum of money he was known to have in the house as the result of a recent sale. King's Farm is in a very isolated position to this day, and it was then even more surrounded by woodland than it is now, so the robbers could anticipate a good chance of getting away, if successful, before their crime became public. There are several versions of the story, the following one being told by Eli Gardiner, an old thatcher of Oakridge, whose father had been a farm labourer working at King's Farm at the time of the occurrence. I give it in his own words:

"Hancocks' little girl was playing in Tunley Lane and saw three men disguising (masking?) themselves in the old lime kiln. She ran to tell her father, but they saw her and ran after her. Hancocks saw them coming and made for home. He jumped the garden fence and got into the house. He had just time to take down his gun, but couldn't load it before they were on him and one of them shot him and thought him dead. Then they looked round and found the money and ran off with it. All the farm labourers were got together and given arms and sent out in couples to find the men, but they got a coach and got away, though they got caught in Gloucester. One turned King's Evidence and was let off; one was hanged, the other one was transported."

The farmer was not killed but was blinded for life. Eli said that when he was a boy he often used to have a chat with old blind Hancocks, who always wore a shade over his eyes. He lived to be over 80. Another version relates that Hancocks' little boy was sitting in the ingle-nook of the wide kitchen fireplace when his father was shot and saw the robbers though they did not notice him. When they were caught he identified them. The robber who was hanged came from a village the other side of Stroud. His wife kept the corpse for more than a week in the cottage charging a shilling for every person who came to look at it!

When the old father died his son gave up the farm and built himself a small house at the bottom of the valley below Sapperton. His two daughters were living there when I came to Oakridge. They are probably still alive but have long since left the district. Another branch of the family was represented by old Hancocks of Lilyhorn, who died childless in 1940. When I saw him he was a very old man. He had recently lost his wife, and his house and furniture were to be sold for the benefit of his father-in-law, to whom he had mortgaged it. Among the furniture were some interesting Jacobean pieces in their original grey oak, not stained or polished as they invariably are in antique shops. He also had a pair of jackboots which were said to have belonged to Cromwell himself and given by him to W. Hancox, and a leather jerkin of even earlier date.

Another more recent tragedy, known as the Oakridge Lynch Murder, was sufficiently notorious at the time for an effigy of the murder to be placed in Madame Tussauds. In this case the son of the farmer at a farm now known as Frampton Court, murdered his father, though, it was said, not without great provocation, as the old man had attacked his wife, but nevertheless was hanged for the crime. This happened recently enough to be still talked about when I was at Oakridge. It was said that the ghost of the murdered man haunted one room at the farm, so this was closed and the doorway bricked up. Later the ghost was exorcised by the parish priest. But there was another sequel later, shewing how a perfectly innocent person can suffer for the crime of another. A friend of Gimson and the Barnsleys bought a cottage at Oakridge and came to live there for a time. He was a man of great charm and geniality and could not understand why his pleasantries failed to produce even a smile from the respectable elderly woman whom he employed as a "daily help". One day he asked her why this was so, whereupon she told him, " I have never felt much inclined to smile since my husband was hanged!"

I was not long enough at Oakridge to get to know many of the villagers well at the time, though, as many of them were in the building trade, I knew them better later on when they were working on buildings for which I was responsible. A friendly little man who was my nearest neighbour and whose wife used to bake cakes for me, told me most of the stories and legends about Oakridge and Bisley. Old Billy Bucknell, a blacksmith and wheelwright in a small way at Tunley, was another source of local information. He was old enough to remember the "hungry 'Forties" when the poor had to live on what he called "barley bangers" eked out with mangels stolen from the fields, an occasional trapped rabbit and tea brewed from ground ivy. He told a story of one poor widow with several children who, yet, at that time, when all the other families were weak with hunger, kept well and strong "just as if she were a lady", much to the surprise and envy of her neighbours. For a long time she refused to explain this to them, but at last was persuaded to

61

tell her secret. She and her family were living on snails! No doubt they were the ordinary or common garden ones, though the large edible snail is occasionally found in the district and is quite common in the Chedworth and Withington woods. They are locally called Roman snails, and it is a coincidence that both the above-mentioned places were the sites of Roman villas, but whether they are indigenous or were, like walnut and chestnut trees, pheasants and other good things, introduced by the Romans, who shall say? Billy Bucknell's favourite hobby was pig-killing and he was generally called in when a pig had to be killed, as he was an expert at it, killing the animal with the utmost dispatch and the minimum of suffering, his fee being invariably the spare rib. His son, Alfred, was Gimson's foreman blacksmith, as fine a craftsman as could be found in that class of work. He could do other things as well, such as wheelwright's work and clock mending, and could play the fiddle. Another son, Joe, could turn his hand to anything in the way of building and many other things besides. For some time he was a miller and the last time I saw him he was building an oven to make malt, so that he could brew his own beer! On Sundays he was a local preacher and cycled miles to fill the pulpit of Methodist chapels in distant villages. At Tunley, too, lived old Mrs. Phelps. When she was a young woman she had mixed the mortar, carried the stones and generally acted as a labourer to her mason husband, in building the tiny cottage in which she lived. There was a deep well of clear water attached to it, and when a friend asked her for a drink of water she told him "Yer can have as much as yer like and welcome, and yer'll find it as cold as charity."

So much for the other side of the valley, as we always call it, for the valley even now is a sufficient obstacle to make communication between those living on the opposite sides of it comparatively rare, and to give a very different outlook to those of each side. At Sapperton our natural shopping centre is Cirencester, while Oakridge people all shop at Stroud as a matter of course. We tend to be conservative in outlook and politics; they used to be radical and now tend to be socialists. These tendencies have probably been in evidence for many centuries, for did not Sir Henry Poole entertain King Charles I at Sapperton, while not long afterwards Cromwell visited his friend Hancox at Daneway?

Chapter IV

SAPPERTON VILLAGE

THE village of Sapperton has changed very little in outward appearance since I first saw it in 1907. Then there was a small cottage instead of the present house at the entrance to the village, a blacksmith's shop where the village hall now stands, and a wheelwright's yard instead of the pair of new cottages to the right of the church. These are the major changes. Minor ones are that the roads were white instead of black, there were no telegraph poles, the gardens were brighter with flowers, while in the winter there were the bright scarlet cloaks worn by the schoolchildren to add a touch of colour at a season when it was most welcome. These cloaks were the gift of Lady Bathurst.

The village is entered by a short length of road from the ancient Salt Way, along which, in the middle ages, pack-horses brought salt from the mines in Worcestershire. On one side of the approach road is a wide strip of greensward bordered by tall trees. This is The Butts, where the villagers once practised shooting with the long bow. Incidentally, the yews in the churchyard are said to have been planted in order to provide a stock of yew for bows. On the opposite side of the road is the large orchard belonging to the Court Farm, a house often mistaken by strangers for the manor house. Immediately beyond The Butts is the Glebe Farm, built shortly before the 1914–18 war, but in the local materials and style. Opposite to it is the Rectory, a good-sized house with stone-mullioned and transomed windows, a house of some age but with 19th century alterations. It has a large garden and two paddocks. Beyond the Rectory is a characteristic Cotswold cottage of the late-Tudor type, while opposite it is the long low building of the Bell Inn, with a skittle alley behind it. Beyond it on the same side are three cottages, and then at the corner opposite the church is a large house, once the wheelwright's, but now divided into cottages. Opposite is the policeman's cottage, and higher up the village hall, built in 1912. We are now at the junction with the main village street which to the right leads past the pair of new cottages to the house Ernest Barnsley built to live in, and a cottage on the opposite side that was his gardener's. A narrow lane bends round the house and continues on down the hill to Dorvel House, built for William Hancox, and on to the now ruined Dorvel Mill at the bottom of the valley. Beyond this is a track through the wood to Henwood Mill, also now a ruin. At the bend of the lane a gate opens to the drives leading to the cottages Sidney Barnsley and Ernest Gimson built for their homes. Returning now to the junction, on the right is the churchyard gate from which the path slopes steeply down between tall yew trees to the church porch. Behind the church a few uneven mounds mark the site of the manor house of the Pooles and Atkins, with a level plateau to the west of them, which was the bowling green of the mansion. Back at the churchyard gate the street to the left follows the crest of the valley in a graceful curve, with cottages and gardens on both sides, some of those on the lower side being approached by a narrow lane joining the street by the village school, a building put up in Victorian times but harmonizing very well with the rest of the village. Beyond the school, cottages continue for about another 100 yards to the top of Daneway Hill, where there are four crossroads, that opposite the village street being the road to Frampton Mansell, that to the right to Daneway and Bisley, and the road to the left, after crossing the Salt Way, leading to the Four Mile Lodge, where it meets the main road from Cirencester to Stroud about a mile away. Behind a small green at the corner of the crossroads is a pair of cottages built by Ernest Barnsley. Beyond them is "Grandmother's Green", a larger patch of grass roughly triangular in shape, on the far side of which is the cottage I now live in and another pair of cottages at the end of the green. Then comes a paddock and beyond it the yards and buildings of the Court Farm, which is entered by a private road, the other end of which ends opposite the Glebe Farm. On the right is a large mound planted with beech trees, the first of a series marking the line of the canal tunnel, of which they are the excavated material. Just beyond this the road crosses the Green Ride, a fine avenue of wych elms extending to the right about half a mile, to the top of the valley, while to the left it becomes the main ride in Lord Bathurst's Park. So much for the geography of the village. Of the buildings that deserve more detailed description I will begin with the church. The dedication is to St. Kenelm, the Saxon boy prince who was murdered by his wicked sister, who had his body hidden in Clent Forest, where it was miraculously found and brought back to Winchcombe, his capital, where an abbey was founded to commemorate him. I will refrain from giving the whole legend, to believe which must have been difficult even in the days of faith. Sapperton was said to have been one of the places where the white oxen bringing his body back from Clent stopped, whereupon a spring immediately gushed out of the hillside, that spring being still called St. Kenelm's. There is nothing recognisably Saxon in the church in its present state, though it may easily be of Saxon foundation. Slight traces of Norman work remain in the North Transept, but it seems probable that the small original church was greatly enlarged and re-built in the 14th century, the date of the tower

67

and spire and the roofs of nave and chancel. The North Transept was altered in Tudor times, probably when the Poole monument, recessed in the east wall, was placed there. This monument is notable for the finely carved Tudor roses on the sides of the arched canopy and for the effigy, resembling in its stiffness, though not in its attitude, the Fettiplace monuments at Swinbrook. The important Jacobean monument to Sir Henry Poole at the north end of the transept, is a fine example, especially interesting for the kneeling figure of Sir Devereux Poole on the left-hand side, who, as the inscription says, "being but of tender age was for his worthiness and valoure knighted in France by Henry IV the French king after his own order and there ended his days and was there buried 1590." On the right-hand side is the figure of the eldest son, in appearance an exact replica of his father. He it was who entertained King Charles I here in 1644. The Pooles sold the Sapperton estate to Sir Robert Atkins at the Restoration. They had other properties, one in Norfolk, where I once found a little country church full of their monuments. Some twenty years ago I became acquainted with a dear old parson who was a lineal descendant of these Pooles. He was then Rector of Quinton, near Stratford-on-Avon, living in a great Victorian rectory fast falling into decay. At the side of the porch there was a bell-pull which had long been out of order. An electric bell and a spring bell contraption on the door were both in the same condition, but on the doorstep was a large and solid hand-bell labelled "Please Ring", which nothing short of an earthquake could have put out of action!

In the South Transept is the imposing monument of Sir Robert Atkins, author of *The Ancient and Present State of Gloucestershire*, who lived at Pinbury, while his father, also Sir Robert, occupied the manor house.

It is probable that it was Sir Robert Adkins, senior, who inserted the large semi-circular headed windows in the church and made some other alterations, including lining the nave walls with ashlar. More alterations were made soon after the first Earl Bathurst bought the estate after the death of the second Sir Robert in 1711. The manor house was pulled down, a great deal of its panelling and other fittings being used to embellish the church. Some idea of what the manor house was like can be obtained from the framed engraving by Kipp hanging in the North Transept, taken from a copy of Sir Robert Atkins' book, but unfortunately Kipp cannot be relied on for very exact detail. Some of the windows from the manor house were built into the sham ruin in the Park, known as Alfred's Hall, where also there is some more of the oak panelling. These windows correspond fairly well with those shewn in Kipps' engraving, but some of his gables look, to say the least, unlikely, while from the liberties he took with the landscape it seems only too probable that the engraving was made from a very rough sketch. One of the coats of arms on the Jacobean cornice of the nave is that of Whittington, that family being related by marriage to the Mansells of Frampton Mansell in this parish.

The village hall was built in 1912 as a gift to the village by Lady Bathurst; Ernest Barnsley was the architect. It is an attractive many-gabled building, built of the local stone and with a stone tiled roof. There is a good-sized hall with a stage, a billiard room, reading room and kitchen. It has always been in constant use, especially in the winter, for dances, plays, whist drives and other entertainments, and the smaller rooms for billiards and meetings of all sorts. The gift has been greatly appreciated by the villagers.

Many of the cottages were built on what was called

"the three life system". Under this arrangement the landlord provided the site and the materials for the house while the tenant provided the labour. The tenant, his son and grandson occupied it rent-free, after which it reverted to the landlord. In one or two of the cottages so built the occupier was still living rent-free in 1912. Being built in this way they were constructed of the materials nearest to hand. The stone for the walls came from the village quarry, and as it was not suitable for stone-mullioned windows or other dressed stonework, wood was used for the windows and the opening spanned by oak lintels. Stone tiles were obtained locally, while the timber came from the woods on the estate and was sawn on the pit at the carpenter's shop. The windows had leaded lights, though many of them have since been replaced with wooden glazing bars. Those cottages built by the more well-to-do tradesmen, such as the wheelwrights and the carpenter, were the largest, but some of the others were very small indeed, consisting of one living-room and a combined larder and store-room on the ground floor and a landing and bedroom above. The main room had a large open fireplace, generally with a bread oven opening into it and forming a semi-circular projection outside. The narrow stairs started on one side of the fireplace and wound up to the bedroom floor. Most of the cottages were detached, with good-sized gardens. Those in groups or pairs had been built under different conditions, usually for agricultural workers, or for the rector's servants. Such is the pair with an inscription stating them to be church cottages, dated 1839. These have stone-mullioned windows and are more consciously architectural in appearance than their humbler neighbours. Then there is a group of cottages towards Frampton known as the "Barracks" which were built to house some of the navvies for the canal tunnel. Two small additions to a tall pair of cottages near the church are also said to have been built for this purpose. The cottages must have been built at varying times from the seventeenth century to the present time, but being built of the same materials, mostly with steeply pitched roofs and gables and to the same plan, they follow the same tradition so closely that the later ones look just as old as the earlier. All are charming in an unostentatious and natural way, the result of the natural taste and traditional methods of their builders, who neither knew nor wanted any other way. In those days villagers learnt many different trades. Most of them could dress stone tiles and dry stone walling was an accomplishment of all farm labourers, so when work was slack on the farm the men were put on to building or repairing the stone walls round the fields, or to build cattle sheds or pigstys. To build a dry stone wall, using the stones for the most part just as they were dug in the quarry with only occasional use of the stone hammer, filling up the space between the two faces evenly with smaller stones and keeping the courses level, requires considerable skill, so that a man who can put up a good dry stone wall is just as capable of building the walls of a house. Actually the walls of many of the cottages were built dry and only pointed in mortar, which in the absence of sand, was made with lime and road drift, collected from the gullies at the sides of the roads. The ground floors of these cottages were paved with squared stone slabs from Ball's Green Quarry, about ten miles away, which was said to have provided stone paving for St. Paul's Cathedral. Up to the 1914–18 war the price at the quarry was 4d. a square foot. After the war the quarry was bought by a company, expensive machinery was installed and much money spent on advertisement and in other ways, with the result that the price went up to 3/- a square foot, very few purchasers were found and the quarry closed, a thing that has happened to many good quarries in the Cotswolds. Up to the time of the war, building was very cheap. Mason's and carpenter's wages were 7d. an hour, labourers 5d., while locally obtained materials were correspondingly reasonable in cost and the difficulty of transport before motor lorries came into use discouraged the use of others. The village carpenter and the wheelwright, or one of the masons, contracted for any work that was needed, Gimson's and the Barnsleys' houses and the village hall being built in this way. Trade Unions had few local adherents, so there were no restrictions preventing masons working as stone-tilers or plasterers if, as was usually the case, they could do the work as well. As an example of the low cost of building then, the two cottages built by Ernest Barnsley above Daneway Hill, which are full-sized cottages, with similar accommodation to that of "Council Houses", but have solid stone walls and stone tiled roofs, cost £400 for the pair. To-day (in 1950) they would cost nearly £2,000 each!

The Court Farm is a large one. Counting the grazing land in the Park that goes with it its acreage is over 1,000. Its large orchard consists mostly of cider apples and perry pears, but it also has several walnut trees. The garden is also large, bounded on the south side by a long ten foot wall, on which much fruit might be grown. The yards and farm buildings are also ample. The house itself has the proportions of an old manor house, but was actually built only about a century ago. For that time it is a good example of Cotswold architecture, but the proportions of the windows, thinness of their stone-mullions and clumsy chimney caps shew the deterioration in taste since the seventeenth century. Inside the contrast is still more marked, the rooms being too high for their size, while their Victorian fireplaces and painted woodwork lack the comfortable proportions of the oak beamed rooms with low ceilings and open fireplaces found in houses of the earlier period. For the last 50 years the farmer has lived in the kitchen wing, the front rooms not even being furnished. The Glebe Farm is much smaller, being only about 100 acres in extent. Before the present house was built, it was a long, low cottage, standing at right angles to the road with a pretty garden containing a well-clipped yew hedge surmounted by a yew peacock, which still remains. There are three other farms in the parish: one at Park Corner, where the old road from Bisley to Cirencester crossed the Salt Way. Here there used to be an inn, but this has been converted into farm cottages. Whitfield, the Methodist evangelist, is said to have held meetings here in the 18th century.

Hailey Farm is on the far side of the Stroud to Cirencester road and about a mile and a half from the village. There are two cottages by the farm and a group of four on the road not far away. These are called Tumbledown Cottages from an accident that happened on the hill in front of them early in the 19th century. A wagoner was sitting on a shaft of his wagon when his horses took fright and ran away down the hill, throwing him off, so that he was crushed under the heavy wheels and killed.

The other farm is Beacon Farm, on the same road but nearer to Frampton Mansell. This is a fairly large house of about the same date as the Court Farm. As its name suggests, it stands on high ground where a beacon was lighted on national occasions.

There are also several outlying cottages in the parish, including lodges in the Park and keepers' cottages.

Daneway lies partly on one side of the stream

73

dividing the parishes of Sapperton and Bisley and partly on the other, but being much nearer Sapperton is included in it for many purposes. At the foot of the hill were the sawmills, chiefly used for converting beech into plane blocks and brush backs. When I first knew it, the proprietor was an elderly man named Job Gardiner, who also sold coal brought up to this point by barge on the canal. His eldest son, as I have mentioned earlier, made chairs for Gimson. His house stood in a very exposed position above the sawmills. Just before the bridge is a cottage belonging to the Canal Company, while on the far side is the Bricklayers' Arms, an inn built for the refreshment of the tunnel navvies. There used to be a large man-trap hanging on the wall near the entrance. Adjoining it is a cottage where at that time lived an old man named Cainey. His proudest possession was a spade guinea, which he had inherited together with its history. The story, as he told it, was that his grandfather happened to be near the entrance to the tunnel one day, just after it was finished, when he saw several gentlemen on the towing path. One of the gentlemen called him up and asked him to guess who he was. Cainey replied that he didn't know, whereupon the gentleman pulled out a guinea from his pocket and told him to look at it, "and he looked at him and he looked at the guinea, and sure as sure the gentleman's face and the face on the guinea were as like as two peas!" "The gentleman" said he was George III and told Cainey to keep the guinea to remember him by. This must have been in 1792, when the King formally opened the tunnel, attended among other local gentlemen by the last of the Hancocks to live in Daneway House. The strange thing about the episode is the little interest that appears to have been taken locally in the King's visit. One can only suppose that no steps were taken to advertise the event and that the villagers simply didn't know of it till old Cainey told them about it afterwards, proudly displaying his guinea! That the King was persuaded to open the tunnel shews what an important piece of engineering it was considered at the time. The tunnel mouth, a picturesque arch in dressed stone surmounted by a battlemented parapet, is a few hundred yards up the canal from Daneway Bridge. Close to it is a cottage in which lived a mason whose duty it was to keep the walls and roof in repair. Two and a quarter miles long, for the most part through solid rock, it must have taxed the limited resources of the engineers of those days very considerably. Shafts were sunk from above about every quarter of a mile, and the stone was raised by pulleys on derricks above them and spread round, forming a series of large mounds, or tumps, as they are locally called, which were planted with beech trees, thus becoming a picturesque feature in the landscape. All the shafts were covered over, except one near the centre of the tunnel, as I realised when a party of us were taken through the tunnel in a barge hired at Daneway, the bargees pushing the barge along with poles on each side. At the other end is Tunnel House, an inn which must have been in great request by the bargees after their strenuous passage. It stands entirely surrounded by Hailey Wood, some half mile from the village of Coates, has a comfortable old-fashioned bar parlour and a large room over for teas, which used to be excellent. There is also an open-air skittle alley. Some time after our voyage, out of curiosity, I examined all the "tumps", finding the open shaft close to and nearly opposite Tumbledown Cottages, protected only by a post and rail fence. As the shaft must be from 200 to 300 feet deep, it suggests an alternative origin for the name given to the cottages.

The Thames and Severn Canal, for which the tunnel

was made, runs from Framilode on the Severn to Inglesham, near Lechlade, on the Thames. The difference in level required an abnormal number of locks, which must have greatly increased the time taken by the barges, towed by strings of donkeys, though it must have been very useful for transporting coal and other heavy materials before the railway came. But its period of prosperity was short. Before 1840 the grandson of the famous Brunel the First, who was the engineer for the canal tunnel, was at work superintending the making of another tunnel in the parish. This time it was for the Great Western Railway, and the debris was left in huge untidy heaps, instead of neat circular tumps planted with trees. This tunnel is about half a mile away from the other, to which it is roughly parallel, but it starts on a higher level and is much shorter, being less than two miles long. One of a pair of outlying cottages in a wood under which it passes is still called "Tommy Shop", a record of its use to serve the navvies during its construction. When the railway was opened, its company promptly bought up the canal and stopped all traffic on it, allowing it to become derelict, but some sixty years later the Gloucestershire County Council acquired it and made a valiant effort to re-establish it. They repaired or replaced the lock gates, dredged the canal, puddled long stretches of it with clay where the water leaked away into faults in the rock, and made reservoirs to store the water to replace wastage. They even built a pumping station near Thames Head, one of the reputed sources of the river which is about four miles from Sapperton, with the result that the Thames now rises some miles lower down! Unfortunately it was to no purpose. The canal was so little used that there was not enough traffic to pay for the cost of upkeep, so the Council had to give up their venture. The barge in which I went through the tunnel was the last one to do so. After old Job Gardiner died, no more coal barges came to Daneway and the canal soon again became derelict above Chalford, to which point it is still used.

In medieval days every village had its mill, the Sapperton Mill being at the foot of the steep lane at the top of which Ernest Barnsley built his house. By that time the mill itself was no longer used and was already partly in ruin, but the picturesque little cottage that had been the mill house was still occupied. Past it led a rough track through Dorvel Wood to a much larger mill about half a mile further on that had been the mill of Daneway Manor. This was Henwood Mill, a partly fifteenth century building, with additions of later date. At that time the only access to it by vehicles was the aforementioned track, but it was quite close to the old pack-horse way from Bisley to Ciren-cester, which, no doubt, had been the route taken by the farmers bringing their corn to be ground in it in earlier days. In spite of its innaccessibility the mill was still used, though the trade had decreased very much in the previous twenty years, and the miller, a cheerful happy-go-lucky man, named Hapgood, had a good deal of time on his hands. We used to go down there to see a tame badger which he kept in one of the outbuildings, but after a few months' captivity it managed to burrow its way under the foundations and escape to the large badgers' earth at the back of the mill, which is still occupied by its kind. After Hapgood's death, the farmer ground his pig-meal at the mill for a few years and there were tenants in the house for a few more, but since then the place has been allowed to fall into complete ruin. It was an interesting building archi-tecturally, having a beautifully worked little fifteenth century chimney at one corner, stone buttresses and other mediæval features, though later additions had robbed it of much of its beauty. When it became ruinous the chimney was carefully removed and now serves a useful purpose at the church. So both mills are now gone and little remains but a few moss-grown stones to shew where they stood.

A thing that struck me forcibly on my first visit to Sapperton was the exceptionally fine trees of many different kinds in and near the village. There was a splendid oak tree 20 feet in girth for some 25 feet in height before it branched out, in the lane below Ernest Barnsley's house. An immense elm, now only a stump, grew just beyond the gate leading to Gimson's and Sidney Barnsley's cottages, while there was a finely shaped plane tree a little further on. There were also some grand walnut trees and a giant Scotch pine in one of the cottage gardens. There were also the ancient yews in the churchyard, well-grown chestnuts of both kinds, wych elms and sycamores, but the dominant note was struck by the beeches in number, size and grace. In all the many woods round the village, beech trees predominate. There are, too, a few enormous old beeches in Sapperton Park, near the parish boundary stone, which must have been there in the time of the Pooles. Oakley Park was thickly planted with beeches by the first Earl Bathurst, a fine legacy to his descendants, starting a tradition which they have kept up ever since. The estate agent, Mr. Robert Anderson, was a well-known authority on silviculture, and in his time no less than 40,000 trees were planted every year, and though many of them were larches the hardwood trees were not neglected. Of the beauty and interesting features of Oakley Park I will say no more here, as it is beyond the parish. Sapperton Park has been a continuation of it ever since the first Earl bought it from Sir Robert Atkins. It is bordered by copses and crossed by the great avenue, but is not thickly planted with trees like Oakley Park, and chiefly consists of meadow land with only a few solitary trees here and there.

Coming as I did from Norfolk, where every wood was placarded with notices against trespassers, it was wonderful to me to have come into a part of the country so beautiful and unspoilt in which I was free

GIMSON BEHIND TREE IN SAPPERTON

to go wherever I wanted. In this corner of Gloucestershire one could walk anywhere where no damage
was done by so doing, and there was an endless variety
of natural beauty to be seen, as well as many interesting
villages, in whatever direction one chose. One could
drop down to the bottom of the valley to follow
the little stream which later becomes the River Frome,
famous for the property in its water to dye scarlet
cloth, up to its source near Brimpsfield, where there
is a ruined castle of the Giffards, close to a little
Norman church. On the way one passed the hamlet
of Caudle Green on one side of the valley and the
village of Syde on the other, both of them charming
and secluded little places, and Syde having a tiny and
picturesque church with a saddleback tower. Or one
could take the Salt Way to Winstone and on to Elk-
stone with its famous Norman church. Or starting
the same way, turn off at Jackbarrow Farm to Duntisbourne Abbots, a picturesque hillside village with
another church with a saddlebacked tower, then following along the bottom of another little valley through
the hamlets of Duntisbourne Leer and Middle Duntisbourne, reach Duntisbourne Rouse. Here there is a
perfect gem of a little church perched on the side of
the valley with evidence in it of the work of every
period of English architecture from Saxon to Queen
Anne. From here it is only a mile to Daglingworth, a
larger village which also has an interesting partly-Saxon
church and a fine circular stone dovecote in the grounds
of the manor house, and so home by Park Corner. Yet
another walk was to follow the Green Lane, as it was
called, starting just outside the village, crossing the
Stroud road and continuing on, between meadows
where mushrooms were plentiful, to Tarlton Downs,
a wild bit of heathy land with clumps of great old
trees, and after crossing the roads to Tarlton and

Rodmarton, arrive at last at Hasleton, a fine old Jacobean house. Beyond this point the old track has long been ploughed up, but it used to lead to Malmesbury and was said to have been a Saxon road. There was a tradition that in the early 18th century a sheepstealer had met his death in this lane in an unusual way. After killing the sheep he was dragging it along with a rope tied round his shoulders. With the object of taking a short cut across the fields, he climbed a high wall when the rope slipped as he was dropping down the far side and the weight of the sheep on the other side of the wall drawing it tight he was hanged.

For a very short walk one could turn off the same Green Lane along the bottom of a little combe teeming with rabbits and with woods on either side to Cassie's Well, a spring enclosed by a low wall and gate. A mound and some loose stones suggest that a cottage once stood here, but I have never been able to find out anything about it, or who Cassie was. In a brier patch on the hillside above, one could occasionally pick a posy of moss roses, thanks to an old pensioner named Tom Gardiner who used to live at Tumbledown, about a quarter of a mile away, whose charming hobby it was to bud the wild briers with them. Turning to the left at Cassie's Well one came to a footpath across the fields to the road about half a mile from Sapperton. Most of the walks described above were fairly long ones that Gimson took me on Saturday afternoons or Sundays. Those we went nearly every day after tea were much shorter and were generally through the woods, starting either along the Leasowes above his cottage, which had been the common strips of cultivated land in the middle ages, or down into the valley and along as far as Pinbury or Edgeworth Mill; or through the village, the High Wood beyond it and a long wood beyond that to near Chapman's Cross and so back by

Lark Hill. Chapman's Cross, by the way, was named after a suicide, buried at the crossroads. There are several other crossroads in Gloucestershire associated with suicides. At one, not far from Winchcombe, was Dabb's Elm, a tree that was said to have grown from the stake driven through the body to prevent his ghost from walking! At Betty's Grave, near Ready Token, the pathetic little grass-covered mound of the grave could still be seen just over the hedge by the cross-roads, but that corner is now the garden of a bungalow and the grave has disappeared.

With so many trees about the village there are plenty of birds of many different kinds. Of the less common ones I have seen in my garden, or in the gardens near by, the lesser spotted woodpecker, hawfinch, redstart, blackcap, tree-creeper, long-tailed tit, coal tit and bull-finch. The green woodpecker is common in the meadows, while you can occasionally see a kingfisher by the stream, and generally be able to watch the dipper bobbing up and down on a stone in the brook. Every now and then a pair of herons come to take toll of the fish in the Pinbury fishpond. The tawny owl nests in the trees in the Rectory shrubbery and the barn owl in the farm buildings, but the little owl has greatly de-creased in numbers. Jackdaws will fill any disused chimney with sticks, and seagulls are as common as rooks on the ploughed fields, and seem to have become permanently land birds. Doubtless the list of rarer birds could be considerably increased by a careful bird watcher, a title to which I can lay no claim.

There are many "local", if not rare, butterflies and moths, such as the Marbled White, at least four kinds of Fritillaries, Common and Green Hairstreak among the butterflies, and Cream Spot Tiger and several of the Hawks among the moths, while Sapperton is famous among lepidopterists as the last place in England

where the large Blue Butterfly was seen and, alas,
caught! It is also a good district for wild flowers. In
the woods can be found the Lily of the Valley, Solo-
mon's Seal, Wild Hellebore, Herb Paris, Daphne,
Bird's Nest Orchid and Deadly Nightshade. In the
meadows twelve varieties of orchis, flax, eyebright,
tormentil, meadow saffron (locally known as Naked
Ladies), and many more.

In the hedgerows, white and purple Sweet Violets,
the large blue Cranesbill, Mountain Cranesbill, Bloody
Cranesbill, Wood Sorrel; while on the dry walls grow
Pennywort, Toadflax, Pellitory of the Wall, and Stone-
crop. Not actually in the parish, but less than ten miles
away, at Oaksey, grows the Snakes' Head Fritillary,
near the Fosse Way the Pasque Flower, and at
Battlescombe the Wild Daffodil. These Gimson used
to always walk over to see when they were in bloom,
but one Spring he was disappointed. He met a group
of people coming away carrying large bunches of buds,
and overheard one of them say, "Isn't it a shame,

FRITILLARIES
Design for candle sconce
by the author.

someone's been and picked all the flowers and only left the buds for us." They had made sure of all the buds, however! A bunch of wild Lilies of the Valley was sent every year to Queen Victoria.

Of wild animals the badger is quite common though difficult to see. Foxes are too common to please the owners of chickens. A most charming sight I was once lucky enough to see was four foxcubs playing like kittens outside their earth, rolling each other over and playing a kind of hide and seek in the bushes round. Another pretty sight was a family of weasels playing on a dry stone wall and running to and fro along the top of an adjoining gate. When I first came to the village there were many red squirrels now, alas, only grey ones. Also at that time there was a considerable herd of fallow deer in Lord Bathurst's Deer Park, but owing, I believe, to the tax put on them by the first Socialist government, they were dispersed. However, quite a number of them escaped into the main Park and have lived a wild life ever since, some of them being seen as far away as Edgeworth on the other side of the valley, while one still occasionally comes across them in the Park or in Hailey Wood. Some years ago I saw a group of five in the Park, one of which was pure white. So beautiful did it look as I glimpsed it between the tree trunks, the trees in their first Spring foliage with a carpet of bluebells on the ground, that it was easy to understand what a hold the white hart had on the imagination of the men of the middle ages, resulting in so many charming legends and fairy tales, not to mention its use in heraldry and, through heraldry, in inn signs.

Chapter V

VILLAGE CHARACTERS

THE Reverend Hugh Douglas Cropper had been appointed Rector of Sapperton in 1884, following the fifty-year-long incumbency of his predecessor, "Parson Pye", as he was locally called. At that time the living was worth £700 a year, and as Mr. Cropper also had private means he could afford to live in his large rectory in considerable style, with a valet, a cook, a housemaid and a coachman-gardener to minister to his needs. He remained a bachelor all his life and was called by some a woman-hater, but the term was actually too harsh to apply to his attitude to women, to whom he was normally polite and courteous. In appearance he was of medium height, plump, and with a large head, rosy gilled and double chinned, with a serious expression, as befitted his responsible position in the village. His hair was white, but his eyebrows were black, while his keen grey eyes were alert to all that went on within their range. Always carefully dressed, he wore a black frock-coat, with grey striped or black trousers, a clerical collar and a top hat. Apart from the collar he might easily have passed for a prosperous company director, except for his foible of wearing a dandelion in his buttonhole, solemnly affirming that it was his favourite flower! When he first came, there was no one else living in the village above the status of working farmer, so he naturally took the leading place in the small community, ruling the village firmly but kindly, taking his duties seriously, and visiting the sick and dying, dispensing to them beeftea, rice pudding and sometimes bottles of port. He never advertised his good deeds and only after his death did it come to be generally known that he had apprenticed

85

several likely youths to useful trades at his own expense. He didn't believe in long sermons and had no aspirations to shine in the pulpit, his sermons generally not lasting more than ten minutes. No friends or relations were invited to stay with him and he seldom went out visiting, so he must have led a very lonely life. He had one old friend from his Brasenose days, whom he used to go to stay with for a few days at Christmas time, but these visits came to an abrupt end, owing to his friend's inhospitable behaviour. It seems that on his arrival at his friend's rectory, for he too was a parson and a bachelor, his host lighted a candle and conducted him upstairs to his bedroom with a jug of hot water, for him to change for dinner. Leading him up to the old-fashioned mahogany dressing table, he pointed out a round water stain on it, remarking severely, "That is what you made with your hot water jug last Christmas." This was enough to break the thin thread of friendship that had lasted since their undergraduate days at Oxford, for it was the last visit Mr. Cropper made to his old friend.

When Gimson and the Barnsleys came to Sapperton, the rector didn't quite know what to make of them. He couldn't undrestand anyone who hadn't got to do so, making furniture with his own hands, as Sidney Barnsley did, or any "gentleman" having workshops for furniture making and smith's work, like Gimson. Besides, they didn't go to church. He was always polite and willing to chat, when he met any of them in the village street, but that was as far as he was prepared to go, while for that matter, they were perfectly content that it should be so. But when the Glebe Farm was re-built, the first tenants were a Mr. Gulley and his wife (I have changed the name for obvious reasons), who came from India, where Gulley had held some minor post in the Indian Civil Service. They went to church regularly, I think, hunted, and from all accounts were "gentlefolk". So without making any very careful enquiries, or waiting till he knew them, he welcomed them with open arms, and the post having just become vacant, made Gulley his churchwarden. The Gulleys on their part had come fully prepared to be the village squire and—within limits—lady bountiful. They considered themselves important people and expected to be welcomed by the County, while in the village they would be respectfully kow-towed to, the boys touching their caps and the girls curtseying. Unfortunately for them, they were very soon summed up as social climbers and made very little headway in local society, while the village, well-behaved as it was, was not in India, so they were treated with no more and no less respect than other people. Even for those days their conception of what they considered to be the lower classes was a very low one, based perhaps on their Indian experience. Keeping a good cellar of wine themselves, they considered the drinking of an occasional pint of beer by a villager to be a wasteful and disgusting habit and told their men so. Now Mr. Cropper saw no harm in the drinking of beer in reasonable quantities. At the "Club" meetings, when he took the chair, beer was the drink as a matter of course, while he himself provided a barrel of beer for the village at the annual Married v. Single cricket match and on other special occasions, just as he provided a large box of fireworks on Guy Fawkes' Day, "When bad men did conspire, to blow up king and parliament, with G.U.N. powdire," as the old saying had it. In fact, he understood the villagers and liked them to enjoy themselves in a natural and reasonable way, so here he disagreed with his new friends. I must now give one or two instances to shew how alien were the Gulleys' ideas to those of an English village.

87

They employed one old man and his son on their small farm and when harvesting started, these men applied for the customary allowance of beer or cider, then a gallon a day. This was against his principles (for them), so he would not give it to them. However, it happened that he had discovered on a shelf in an out-building a small barrel of home-made blackcurrant wine, left by mistake, perhaps, by the previous tenant. Assuming that this was a harmless teetotal beverage, he gave it to them for their harvest drink. As it happened, this was some of "the right stuff" as the men said afterwards; it had probably been well laced with brandy and had had plenty of time to mature. In fact, if he had given them a dozen bottles of port from his own cellar, it would have had much the same effect. As everyone knows, harvesting is thirsty work, so the men helped themselves freely from the little barrel, with the result that, towards evening, the old man became so unsteady that he fell off the wagon and broke his leg. There was no telephone in those days, so the son got out his bicycle to ride to Cirencester to fetch a doctor, but in spite of his anxiety about his father's accident, he found himself getting more and more sleepy and less and less able to control his bicycle. He managed to steer a zigzag course for the first two miles, by which time he had forgotten altogether about the reason for his ride and, deciding to have a rest, lay down under a tree by the roadside and promptly went to sleep. When he woke up very early next morning, he was perfectly sober but with no recollection of how he came to be two miles from home; so he mounted his bicycle and pedalled back to his cottage, where he was quite unable to answer his wife's searching questions of where he had been all night! When all the facts of the case came out, the general opinion was that it was disgraceful of Gulley to have given such intoxicating drink to his men, all the more as his views on drinking by the working classes were well-known. Another incident that didn't help to make them more popular occurred at the festivities for the Coronation of King George V. Mrs. Gulley presided at the open-air tea party to all the children, who duly arrived in their best clothes, their faces and hands clean and shining, and were seated round the trestle tables, enjoying the good things provided for the occasion. All village children have a way of calling each other by nicknames, or of shortening longer names to one syllable, regardless of the sometimes curious effect. To each other they were Day, Phil, 'Erb, and so on, as the case might be. It so happened that at Mrs. Gulley's end of the table there was a small boy named Godfrey, sitting next to a little girl named Cynthia, and when Mrs. Gulley heard some other child urging "Sin" to pass "God" the cake, she was so horrified that she got up and left the table, loudly declaring that they were all little heathens, which naturally did not please their mothers, who took them to church and sent them to Sunday school and did their best to bring them up according to their lights, as proper little Christians!

These incidents the Rector deplored, but they did not affect him personally. For more than thirty years he had been undisputed autocrat of the little community. When he first came, there had been some resentment about his banishment of the band from the church, but a compromise had been effected whereby the band met at the corner of the common every Sunday, the estate men fell in behind it, the band struck up and the procession marched to the churchyard gate, where the band dispersed to put away their instruments before entering the church, "and if anyone didn't turn up, there was a shilling docked off his wages" as my informant told me. All this had come to an end some years before. After that, village life had gone smoothly enough. Class barriers were formidable matters in his earlier days and he never unbent to any of his parishioners, but he distributed the Gift Bread that was part of the Atkins Charity fairly, was unostentatiously generous to the needy, was felt to have the good of the village at heart and had come to be generally respected and even admired. He disliked changes of any sort and it worried him considerably to have his villagers upset by the bad manners and sheer stupidity of these newcomers. By this time he had a personal grievance against them, too. Soon after their arrival he had lent Gulley the church register, which contained a number of interesting entries, though they did not go back so far as those of many other village churches. Some six months later he asked him to return it, but whether Gulley had mislaid the book, or thought that as churchwarden he had a right to keep it, I don't know. At any rate he refused to return it. The Rector then put his request in writing, but the letter was returned unopened. Mr. Cropper then took it himself, but being refused admittance, threw it in through an open window, but it was again returned unopened. This sort of thing went on for several weeks and the old man worked himself up into such a state of worry and anger at the Gulley's indefensible behaviour that his mind became unhinged and he had to go away for some time, leaving his duties in the hands of a curate. Meanwhile, to the relief of the whole village, the Gulleys had departed. Mrs. Gulley confided to an acquaintance that she had come in for a legacy, including a barouche and "Sapperton was no place for a barouche." It is hardly necessary to say that in this, even if in nothing else, Sapperton entirely agreed with her! Poor old Mr. Cropper did not survive much longer. He came back to the Rectory for a few months in charge of a nurse, but the events of the last year or two had completely broken him up and he died at the age of 75, having been Rector of Sapperton for 34 years. By the irony of fate the poor old man, reputed woman-hater as he had been for so many years, was found to have no clean nightshirt at the last, his valet having absconded with all his linen the day before, so his body was laid out in a woman's shift provided by the nurse.

The village band lasted for nearly twenty years after it had been banished from the church in 1887. Besides the Sunday procession it was in great demand in this and neighbouring villages, for weddings, harvest and other festivities. It played at Gimson's and Sidney Barnsley's weddings, but it was not many months after that it came to a sudden and dramatic end. It was playing outside a house at the neighbouring village of Daglingworth, where there was a wedding party, one dark, moonless, autumn night when there was half a gale blowing. It had been "big market" day in Cirencester, and a farmer, who had stayed late drinking with his friends, was driving home in his high gig accompanied by his daughter. The fact that he was "drunk as a lord" didn't signify, as the old horse knew his way home and was making his way there at a good spanking pace. The horse may have been deaf, or else the high wind blowing from behind him prevented him from hearing the band. They themselves were making far too much noise to hear anything coming in time to get out of the way, so before they realized what was happening they were being knocked over like ninepins. Somehow the horse managed to put his foot through the big drum and then took fright and ran away carrying one small boy, whose trousers had got caught in the step of the gig, several yards before he was dropped off. The horse then ran up a bank, overturning the gig and tipping out the farmer and his daughter on the roadside. Fortunately no one was killed. One bandsman had a broken arm, two others broken ribs and others minor injuries. It was, of course, before the days of people suffering from "shock", otherwise no doubt the farmer's daughter and the small boy, if no one else, would have been recorded as cases. Besides the big drum several other instruments were more or less seriously damaged, but no doubt the band would have got over the unfortunate affair if it had ended there. Unluckily, the farmer was advised to bring a case against the band for obstructing the King's highway, so the band had to consult their lawyer and cross-sued the farmer for assault and battery. Their slender resources soon melted away in lawyer's fees, while the farmer went bankrupt from the same cause. The band never played again, but some of the instruments remained, and probably still remain. Occasionally a very solemn elderly man with grey side whiskers of almost the Dundreary pattern, named Albert Arkell, was to be seen at the village hall at dances, gently sawing away at a monster 'cello (or bass viol?), but if any sound did emerge from it, it was drowned by the piano! He was the only member of the old band who could be persuaded to play—or at any rate appear—in public after the catastrophe, but I have at various times seen other instruments which had belonged to it, including the big drum, which can't have been damaged beyond repair.

After the Rector and the farmers (not including Gimson and the Barnsleys, who were comparatively newcomers), the most important man in the village was Richard Harrison, the wheelwright, whose workshops and yards backed on to Ernest Barnsley's garden. He was a shortish plump little man, with a face reddened by exposure, small, humorous blue eyes and a tight mouth hiding entirely toothless jaws—he said he could chew very well with his gums, given time. His scanty hair and slight side whiskers were reddish fading to white. He always wore an apron and a cloth cap. His wife was a thin little woman with a long face, who bore an extraordinary resemblance to Dan Leno when made up as a cockney woman, as I remember him on the music hall stage. Richard was rather deaf, and to people he didn't want to hear, would put his hand to his ear and say "Wat, surr", or "Watt, marm", till they tired of trying to get him to answer them, but with other people got the gist of what they had to say easily enough. If ever a man loved his work, old Richard did. He seemed to live for nothing else, starting work at 6 in the morning and often working as long as it was light in the evening, or at any rate pottering about the shops, seeing all was in order for the next day. When I knew him he only had four men working for him, not many years before he had had up to a dozen, including his younger brother John, who was said to have been the best wheelwright of them all, but he died suddenly three years before. Richard watched his men's work—they were all sons, nephews or cousins that were left—most closely, never letting any slipshod work or faulty material pass. To anyone who really appreciated his craft he enjoyed explaining the reason for using oak for the spokes and elm for the hub and felloes of a wheel, why ash was better for shafts and that the stop-chamfering that added so much to the appearance of a wagon, was only, or at any rate mostly, to reduce the weight where that could be done without reducing the strength. His wagons had bright red (red lead) wheels, shafts and under-carriages, with yellow bodies. "I allus paints my wagons the colour of the carn, Sir", he would say.

Apropos of his standard of good workmanship, he had an anecdote about a wheelwright he went to see in a village a few miles away, who was making a wagon. Old Richard saw something suspicious, and pointing to it asked what it was. "Oh, that's just a bit of putty," said the man, "just as good as oak where it is," to which old Richard countered, "Why not make the whole wagon of putty, then?" When a wagon was finished and painted red and yellow, it still needed to have the name of the owner painted on the dashboard, generally with some ornament of wheat sheaves each side of the lettering. This was "special" work which a man came from Chalford, three miles away, to do. He had the peculiarity (if that is the right word?) that he could only do his best and most delicate work when he was half drunk, so they always kept a bottle of whiskey ready for him. His work when done never seemed to me to be very "special"—certainly his skill with the brush bore no comparison to the wheelwright's skill with the drawknife, but they admired it and thought him a great artist.

Richard's brother John had died before my time. He had kept the Bell Inn and his widow stayed on there for a few years after his death. When she had put by what she considered enough to keep her in reasonable comfort for the rest of her days, she retired to a cottage near mine. Eliza Harrison was a superior type of old lady, independent and with strong prejudices. Short, plump and round-faced, with dark hair only slightly streaked with grey, she was always neatly dressed in black and wore a small black bonnet. We often used to watch her taking her three or four fowls for an airing on the green, on which occasions she was always glad to have a chat, especially about old times in the village. She well remembered old Thomas Fisher, the village centenarian, and gave me photographs of him and another old couple, Jonas and Esther Workman, who had died about thirty years previously. Perhaps she had not expected to live so long, or had miscalculated her expenses, but when she was well over 80 she found that something would have to be done to eke out her savings, so being too proud to accept parish relief, she opened a small general shop, the earnings from which kept her for the few more years she had to live.

The carpenter's workshop was next door to the

JONAS and ESTHER WORKMAN

95

wheelwright's. Arthur Gardiner was a man of middle
height and a large waist measurement. He wore a
heavy moustache over a half-open humorous mouth,
while nature waged a perpetual war with him over his
chin. His father had had a bushy black beard, which
nature evidently intended that he should inherit.
Arthur preferred not to have a beard, but wasn't
going to bother to shave every day, so as a rule Sunday
was the only day his wife could feel reasonably proud
of him. He was happy-go-lucky about his clothes, too,
and wore neither collar nor tie on weekdays, and a
bowler hat that a tramp wouldn't have envied him.
Always cheerful, good-natured and easy-going as he
was in many ways, he was an excellent workman, with
the skill and traditional instinct inherited from his
father and grandfather. He knew all the qualities of
the English timbers, their special requirements in
seasoning and their use to the best advantage when
seasoned. Though he had no ambition to be a builder,
he had the ability to organise building work, and when
he could be persuaded to take a contract, managed his
men admirably and the work was well done and
reasonably. Two or three years after I came to
Sapperton, Job Gardiner, the proprietor of the sawmills at Daneway, died, and his sons decided to set up
elsewhere, so Arthur Gardiner took over the business
and moved down to the comfortable-sized house there.
I happened to be doing some wood-carving at the
time, making some little carved and painted figures for
Miss May Morris, for Kelmscott Manor, so I rented
his vacant workshop at Sapperton from him. He
hadn't bothered to clean out much of his stock-in-trade,
so although the workshop had a large window with a
cheerful outlook the atmosphere inside was rather
macabre, owing to the many accessories of the undertaking side of his business. Thickly covered with dust

on a shelf above my head were large cardboard boxes labelled "men's and women's shrouds", while hanging on nails were stamped metal coffin ornaments (doubtless from Birmingham) painted black and of atrocious design, with inscriptions in raised letters, such as "Abide with Me" and "Nearer my God to Thee". Richard Harrison and Arthur Gardiner were in friendly rivalry over the undertaking business, which both looked on as a profitable sideline. The wheelwrights were proud of their oak or elm coffins made to a special "fishtail" design of their own, the sides having a double curve which required considerable skill to make, while Arthur kept to a more conventional type, but equally well made. Arthur's brother, always known as 'Erb Gardiner, a tall ungainly young man, used to drop in and watch me at work, sometimes. He confided in me that he liked the undertaking business well enough for the most part, but when his brother made him sit on a coffin that was a little too small, to close the lid, it gave him the creeps to hear the bones crunch! I very much doubt whether Arthur ever used any of the Brummagen coffin ornaments, which were probably samples foisted on him by some commercial traveller. It is these people, more than anything else, who have corrupted the inherited good taste of country folk. Glib tongued and flashily dressed, they display their trashy wares to the small tradesmen, urging them to be "in the fashion" and "up-to-date", pouring sarcasm on the sound, well-made and often beautiful productions made in the old traditional way, the shopkeepers in their turn picking up their arguments to persuade their customers.

The rest of the men living in the village were either woodmen, men on the staff of the estate for building repairs, farm labourers, railwaymen and policemen. The policemen were generally moved on elsewhere after four or five years and were out on their rounds most of the day, so I did not see much of them, but most of them were good gardeners. I saw very little of the railwaymen either. There was a long stretch of the Great Western main line to Gloucester and beyond in the parish, including a long tunnel, and two of them manned the signal box at one end of this. The others were platelayers, one of whom was Jasper Green, a short man with curly grey hair, a flowing moustache and an imperial, which gave him a distinctly Yankee appearance. Another, Tom Cobb, son of Thomas Cobb, the keeper who lived at Daneway, told me some of the particulars I have narrated about the band. His garden was always bright with flowers all through the Spring and Summer, culminating in a grand display of dahlias in the Autumn, though usually the men at that time grew the vegetables and left the flowers to their wives. Now more of the men are interested in flower-growing, but most of the younger women are not interested in gardening of any kind.

Of the farm labourers, Raymond Midwinter was the one I knew best, as he lived in a cottage only a few yards from my gate. A powerful well-built man, with dark hair and side whiskers, he always wore corduroy trousers tied with a strap just below the knees, with a coloured handkerchief tied round his neck instead of a collar, and talked very slowly, in the local dialect. He worked for the same master, Mr. Chamberlain, at the Court Farm, all his life, coming with him from Hankerton, near Malmesbury, when he first took the farm. He was cowman, but as there was not a large enough herd cf cows on the farm to take all his time, he also looked after the kitchen garden, laid hedges and made hurdles for the shepherd's use. In his spare time he cut the hair of most of the boys and girls in the village. Another accomplishment of his was water-divining, which he did his best to teach me, but with no success—the forked twig wouldn't turn in my hands, even over a well! With him, however, there was no doubt about it turning and he had fixed the best position for sinking wells in some scores of places, estimating the depth to water level within a foot or two, and as he generally got a sovereign for his trouble, it was quite a useful side-line for him. Ray liked his little joke, however old. Leaning over the garden wall watching me fix my runner bean poles, using some of last year's ones to save getting new, he would say in his slow drawl, "They be'ans 'on't grow on old sticks, Sir." If I rose to the bait and asked him why, he would chuckle and say, "Well, yer see, Sir, they do grow on their own stalks like." He would make the most amazing, not to say amusing, shots at words unfamiliar to him, and I remember on one occasion when he was asked how his daughter, who had gone to service in the next village, liked the parson there, he said, "Ooh, 'e be a very funny sort of man; 'e be one of these chalybeate priests, wot burns innocents."

Another near neighbour was old William Simmonds, who worked at the Downs Farm at Frampton, keeping the carts and wagons in order and making ladders, cattle troughs and such farm furniture. He was a widower at this time, and I went to his cottage one evening to ask him to make me a ladder, finding him busy peeling mushrooms. "Ah," he said, "I be wunnerful fond of musherooms, so they be done proper. I just cooks 'em on a hot iron over the fire; they be good that way, leastways, I think so, but there, everyone to his likin's as the old 'ooman said when 'er kissed the cow." He was cooking them on a sort of girdle that he had made himself, as they are not in general use in this part of England.

Harry Allen had the shepherd's traditional skill in

forecasting the weather, but when the radio was introduced into the village, all he would say when asked what it was going to be, was "They tells me as it says on the wireless that it's goin' to rain", or whatever it might be. However, after a long series of depressions over Iceland (always mentioned by the announcer with such veneration), had resulted in quite different weather on the Cotswolds to that prophesied in the weather forecast, he became more sceptical of the radio and began to notice again the natural phenomena on which he used to rely. An apparently infallible indication could be obtained by noticing the behaviour of the mist in the valley. Not, of course, that there was always a mist there, but pretty frequently you could see in the evening white mist half filling the valley. If it gradually dispersed, moving down the valley towards Chalford, you could be pretty sure that the next day would be fine, but if it moved the other way, gradually rising and hiding the top of Dorvel Wood on the opposite side, Harry would murmer, "When the mist climbs up the hill, it sure will come back with a swill", and so it did, whatever the wireless forecast to the contrary.

One of the woodmen, old George Cook, a sturdy old man with reddish side whiskers, used to say he would give sixpence to anyone who could find a weed in his garden. For several years he was landlord of the Bell Inn as well as working in the woods. Not many months after he had become licencee, two of his nephews from a village the other side of Cirencester called in one day to see him, and in course of conversation enquired how he found the business. "Oh, not so bad," says George.

"Has its ups and downs, I suppose?"

"Oh, no; very steady, very steady indeed. I'll tell you how I does it. As soon as I've had my tea I goes down to the cellars an' I draws off as many pints as I reckon'll be wanted. Then, when closing time comes, if it's all gone I goes to bed, and' if it isn't I just sits up and drinks it!"

He was a very strong man, of whom it was said that he and his son together could carry a ton of wood home on their shoulders, after the day's work. Incidentally, his language was as strong as his muscles! The woodmen were allowed to bring home for their own use wood that they had cut in the dinner-hour. The villagers were allowed to have the fallen "dead" wood in the Park and woods, and could cut wood in the common left to the village by Sir Robert Atkins, so very few of them burnt any coal. I have already mentioned the Gift Bread which was also a bequest of Sir Robert's, who had left a sum of money, the interest on which was to be used to buy bread through the winter months for the distribution to the poorest villagers. Where their incomes were so much the same, it was not easy to decide who should have it, and in other ways the wording of the bequest was rather obscure, but on the whole there was little dissatisfaction with the way Mr. Cropper interpreted it.

Of my immediate neighbours, living in the two small cottages forming with mine the group called Bachelor's Court, Thomas Nash, who lived in the cottage nearest the gate, was a woodman. He left for his work early in the morning, returning in the evening with a "stick" of wood over his shoulder. After that we usually saw very little of him, as he had no friends who called on him except once every few months, his brother Jack. The pair were a great contrast, for while Tommy was heavily built, dark and rather gloomy by nature, Jacky, as he was always called, was small and thin and wiry, with fair wispy hair and moustache and grey dreamy eyes. He wore a very ancient bowler hat and patched and torn clothes, rather too big for him, probably cast-offs given him by one of his employers. He was the kindest, sweetest-natured and lightest-hearted man that could be found; a great favourite with children, for he had all the natural gaiety and irresponsibility of a child himself, spending a great deal of his time just wandering about in the woods watching birds and animals. Generally he was accompanied by half a dozen school children, to whom he loved to shew the haunts of foxes and badgers, the squirrels' drey or the nests of the more uncommon birds. Of course he was obliged to do a little work from time to time, but his wants were few and he paid no house-rent, for he was a good worker, helped with the harvesting and threshing and such jobs paid "by the piece" as hedging and dry-walling, didn't smoke or drink, so the farmers let him "sleep rough" in their barns or outhouses. The more staid among the villagers hardly knew what to make of him, the general opinion being that he had "got a screw loose somewhere", but he was so obviously harmless that they trusted their children with him without misgiving. In his comings and goings he was mysterious, but there was nothing consciously secretive about him and he would answer questions with perfect frankness and in considerable detail, if he was questioned in a friendly way. The time he spent watching birds and animals was from sheer love of nature. It seemed as if he enjoyed a blackbird's song more than other people, pitied more the timidity of the hare, appreciated more the cunning of the fox, or the secretiveness of the badger, so he earned just enough to keep himself alive, and gave up the rest of his time to what he really cared for—the life of the woods and valleys he loved so well. What happened to him in the end, I never heard. He just didn't turn up as usual one Summer and was never seen here again. There had always been something vague and unsubstantial about Jacky, and it seemed a fitting climax to his shadowy existence that he should depart rather like the Cirencester ghost in Aubrey's *Miscellanies*, that "vanished in a delicate odour and with a most melodious twang." My other next-door-neighbour was Billy Fisher, a very old man with a bushy white beard, which he had worn ever since he came back from the Crimea, for he had fought in that war that had produced such a change in hirsute fashions, though no doubt at that time his beard was not a white one. He was an impressive figure but quarrelsome and bad-tempered. The village nurse told me that when his wife lay dying on the sofa in their kitchen, she saw Billy taking his best clothes out of the chest and hanging them in front of the fire. "Billy," quavered the old lady, "what are you airing your blacks for?"

"Woman," said the old man, "d'ye think I wants to catch me death of cold seeing you buried?" after which it is hardly surprising that she turned her face to the wall and died that same day. Such callousness, at such a time, is hard to understand, but by all accounts it was quite in keeping with Billy's character. He himself only lived about six months after we came to live next door to him. Being a Crimean veteran he had been promised a military funeral, so a company of the Gloucestershire Yeomanry were sent out from Cirencester to fire a last salute over his grave.

His brother, Freddy Fisher, was also an old soldier, but being several years younger had been too late for the Crimean War and had fought in Burma. A tall, loose-limbed old man, he was fond of his pint of beer and generally managed to get put in charge of the barrel provided for the annual cricket match. At the end he was taken to the workhouse, where they insisted on his having a bath. "I never wash what's kivered," he protested! But the regulations had to be obeyed, the result being, as has frequently happened before in like cases, that he developed pneumonia and died within a few days. Both Billy and Freddy were the sons of Thomas Fisher, whose photograph I have, shewing him in the broad brimmed hat, smock frock and worsted stockings, which were the customary clothing of farm labourers in his time. He lived to the great age of 106, but had been dead more than ten years when I came to Sapperton.

I wish I could remember more about the old people, so many of whom were still alive at that time. Most of them had endured the hungry 'forties as children and they had much more strongly developed characters than the generations that followed them. I used to occasionally jot down any of their remarks that happened to strike me as worth recording, but according to no set system and only at odd times, for my own amusement. Now it is too late, for that generation has gone, and the present elderly people in the village, few of whom were born in it, or would live in it for preference, have other interests. It is a case of "other times, other manners", but I can't help regretting the old faces, the old wisdom, and the old ways of life in the village as I knew it sixty years ago.

Chapter VI

THE YEARS BEFORE THE WAR

BY the time the alterations were finished at Water Lane House, a cottage was vacant at Sapperton for me. It was really two small cottages with a doorway joining them on the ground floor only. There was a larger garden than I needed, but Mrs. Cobb, who came daily and cooked my mid-day meal for me, arranged for her husband to grow vegetables on it and supply me with all I needed. In one cottage there was a large brick oven, opening out of the six feet wide fireplace, so I was able to make my own bread, as well as other things at times. I once cooked a turkey and a goose together in it—both to perfection. Gimson gave me a copy of Cobbett's *Cottage Economy*, so I made my bread to the instructions in it. I should have liked to have brewed my own beer, too, but lacked the utensils. Nearly every cottage in the village used to have one of these brick ovens, but most of them have been done away with, as the villagers preferred open ranges. To heat a brick oven, you have to burn in it two good-sized faggots of wood, the smoke coming out through the oven door and then up the chimney flue. While there is any smoke, the interior of the oven is blackened, but once the wood is all consumed, leaving only a few hot embers, the walls and top of the oven become quite clean. It is then time to rake out the embers with a long-handled hoe and put in the bread, or whatever else is to be cooked. As it is much too hot to go near the oven, this is done with an oven peel, a sort of long wooden spade. The food is left in the oven for several hours until the oven has cooled down. I used to heat the oven on Saturday evening and take the bread out on Sunday morning, and it was never

105

over or under-done. Everything cooked in a brick oven is invariably delicious—provided, of course, that the material is good in the first place—nothing is burnt, meat is tender, retaining its juices and flavour. My bread, made with stone-ground wholemeal flour, kept fresh for a fortnight. Of course, it was hot work heating the oven and raking out the embers, but it was great fun doing it and the result made it well worth while. Now that I was at Sapperton I could get to the workshop comfortably by 9 o'clock each morning, and as I no longer had three miles to walk each way, morning and evening, I was glad to join Gimson in his walk after tea each fine day. Generally, too, we went for a longer walk on Sunday morning. I soon had a companion at the cottage, as Walter Gissing, a son of George Gissing, the novelist, who had died some years before, came as a pupil to Gimson in 1910. Gissing had had an unhappy childhood, seeing little of his father and nothing of his mother, and had been brought up in Yorkshire by two maiden aunts. He inherited much of his father's rather gloomy view of life, being at times subject to fits of depression, but he enjoyed working with Gimson and was quick to pick up details of any work he was given to do. Passionately fond of music, he spent most of his evenings in Cirencester, where Mr. Gibbons, the gifted organist of the Parish Church, took a kindly interest in him. After a year at Sapperton he spent some months under William Weir to learn the methods of the Society for the Protection of Ancient Buildings, for which Society Weir was the principal architect, having been trained for the work by Philip Webb; then he came back to superintend the building of two cottages that Gimson had designed for Miss Morris at Kelmscott, which work he did admirably. His promising career was cut short when he was killed in the First World War.

Algernon Gissing, his uncle and guardian, who came down to see him occasionally, was a very different type of man to his brother. A cheerful, bustling little man, a prosperous solicitor, he had made up his mind to become famous, like his brother, as a novelist, and had published several three-volume novels, which neither the critics nor the public appreciated. Fortunately, towards the end of his life he realized that writing novels was not his forte and wrote instead a quite charming little book, called *The Footpath Way in Gloucestershire*, about the North Cotswolds, which he knew well and could write about in an interesting way.

Another pupil who came about the same time and lodged where I had first done, at Frampton Mansell, was Basil Young, who came from the North of England, but had a brother living at Fairford. Of independent means, he was interested in blacksmith's work, but more as a hobby than anything else. We had some similar tastes and enthusiasms so he and I became good friends and I often walked over to see him in the evenings, but I have neither seen nor heard from him since he left the district. Gimson designed a delightful house for him at Budleigh Salterton, rather similar in appearance to his own cottage, but being in Devon, with walls of cob instead of stone, for which Young acted as his own builder.

I also saw more of Ernest and Sidney Barnsley and their families, and a year later became engaged to Mary, Ernest Barnsley's eldest daughter. It was a long engagement, and as it happened I was away from Sapperton most of the time. I was sent down to Muchelney, in Somerset, to look after the repairs to the 14th century Priest's House, for the Society for the Protection of Ancient Buildings, staying at the little town of Langport, two miles away and cycling to my work each day. In the evenings and week-ends I

107

explored the country round, in which were many pleasant little towns and villages, many with fine perpendicular churches with their characteristic Somerset towers. Once, near High Ham, I came to a signpost, one arm of which directed me to Beer and the other to Stout, villages or hamlets nearby! When the work at Muchelney was finished, I spent a few months at Sapperton again before going off to Salle, in Norfolk, to look after the repairs to the church, under William Weir. The church at Salle is a large and magnificent fifteenth century building which was built by John of Gaunt, with a fine hammer-beam roof with life-sized angels standing on the hammer-beams and a typical Norfolk-painted rood screen. As was usual in work for the S.P.A.B., no builder was employed, the men having been trained for the work by Weir, so I gained valuable experience by watching them at work. There was another fine church at Cawston nearby. I was surprised to find that witchcraft still flourished in Norfolk at that time, almost as strongly as it had done in the days of Sir Thomas Browne. A reputed witch had died at Salle only the year before, while at Crostwick one was still living and kept her broomstick (a besom) propped against her door post. She was reputed to have cast spells on certain people in the village, preventing them from leaving their premises, and to have caused the death of cattle belonging to people who had offended her, in fact, the usual vague charges.

After three months at Salle I returned to Sapperton to get married. My parents, brother and sisters came down, and three old Cambridge friends of mine, one

Opposite - WEDDING PHOTOGRAPH
NORMAN JEWSON and MARY BARNSLEY 1911
Back Row: L. - R. Mr. W. Jewson, Best man, Mary, Norman, Ethel Barnsley, Ernest Barnsley. Sitting: Mrs. W. Jewson, Grace Barnsley Nellie Barnsley, Mrs. E. Barnsley.

109

of whom acted as best man. The old Rector hurried through the service at great speed, and it seemed to me that Mary and I were made man and wife in record time. After the wedding, we took train to London and then on to Norfolk to get back to Salle, where we stayed at a farm nearby till the work was finished. Then we returned to Sapperton, living at first in the same small cottage, while the larger cottage, which we have lived in ever since, was being altered and repaired. This cottage faces on to the village green and is one of the largest in the village, having been the Glebe Farmhouse till about forty years before we took it. Since then it had been occupied by a handsome old man with a long white beard, and his sister, the son and daughter of Farmer Coates, as their father had always been called. The sister having died, the old man went to live with relatives, so the cottage became vacant and I was allowed to rent it. Farmer Coates had added a stone porch and had planted a yew on each side of the gate, which had grown up and been trimmed into an archway. He had also planted two tall yews that had been clipped into a series of yew cheeses, surmounted by yew peacocks, and had laid out the small garden in the front of the cottage with flower beds, edged with box. I was told that his son had been allowed a reduction in the rent for so long as he kept the yews clipped, and they were in excellent order.

At right angles to the main cottage were two very small ones, made out of old stable buildings, while on the opposite side was a large shed that had been built as a slaughterhouse, but was now my coal and wood shed. The cottages were occupied by two old widowers, one of whom was a pensioner, the other a woodman working for the estate. Later on, when these cottages became vacant, I was allowed to add them to mine, but at first they shared the little garden in front. At the back I had a good-sized vegetable garden, which, having belonged to a farmer, had been well-manured and had a good depth of top-soil, while the other cottages had gardens above it. The three cottages together were known as Bachelor's Court, but though our advent made the name a misnomer we kept it. Inside, our cottage had one good-sized sitting-room and a smaller one, with outbuildings at the back. The main sitting-room had a stone floor and a large open fireplace. The staircase twisted up in the thickness of the wall by the side of the fireplace and was so narrow that it was impossible to get a chest of drawers up or down, so I had a new staircase made at the side of the smaller sitting-room. When this was done it was possible to get the two large chests belonging to old Coates down (they must have been made in the bedroom, unless a window was taken out to get them up), and our bedroom furniture upstairs. The garden in front needed no alteration, but that at the back was completely bare and had no paths, even, so walls, hedges and gravel paths had to be arranged and fruit trees and bushes planted. William Cobb, who did the work for me, was a most able man, an excellent gardener, who, having worked on some big engineering contracts in his younger days, could level a lawn or lay paving with accuracy and economy. Till he was about fifty he had worked in other parts of the country, but had now retired to his native village, taking on the humble job of roadman for the District Council. He had a curious implement called a breast plough, which he used to cut away the turf at the sides of the road, and for other odd jobs. In the mid-nineteenth century and earlier, when much of the land that had formerly been sheep downs was enclosed and broken up for growing corn, the breast plough was extensively used to cut off the turf, which was then collected into heaps, dried in the air and then burnt to ashes, which were spread over the ground and ploughed in. The ground was then sown for wheat, exceptionally fine crops resulting. The process was called Burn Baking. This was in his grandfather's time, and the breast plough had come down to him as a family heirloom. So, too, had the big drum which he had played in the village band, the disastrous end of which I have already related. One of his brothers was a gamekeeper, living in the kitchen wing at Daneway House. Like the other four or five keepers on the estate, he always wore the dark green velveteen jacket with brass buttons embossed with the Bathurst's coat of arms which was their livery, with corduroy breeches and leggings, the jacket having a pocket large enough to hold a rabbit or a pheasant.

William Cobb, being employed regularly on the roads, I engaged Alfred Meecham, an old man of between 70 and 80, to help me with the garden. He always worked for 2/6 a day, "no more and no less." It was what he had always had and all he wanted. He was a steady and methodical worker, so tidy and thorough in everything he did that it was a pleasure to watch him working. None of his time was wasted, so that although his movements were deliberate, he got through far more work in a day than most younger and more active men, while though he liked to have someone to talk to, he never stopped work to talk. He appreciated the good soil in my garden compared with that of others in the village, of one of which he said, "Now that garden wouldn't grow weeds even, not to perfection, however." Like most of the older genera-tion he had a habit of adding "however" or "what-ever" to the end of nearly every sentence. When he was a young man he had been employed by the Company to row through the canal tunnel every day, to see that the roof was safe and report any signs of weakness in it. The tunnel was too narrow for two barges to pass, so, he told me, it was arranged that barges going upwards towards the Thames should have the right-of-way till mid-day, those going the opposite way having preference after that time. He also told me a story of a bargee whose wife had been "giving him too much tongue" persuading her to step off on to the small landing stage at the middle of the tunnel on some pretext and taking his barge on, leaving her to be picked up by the next one, while he waited for her in the comfortable bar at the Tunnel House. As it happened no other barge passed in that direction till the next day, so by the time his good lady arrived at Tunnel House he was too well fortified with beer to appreciate the tale of her adventures as well as she would have liked!

Another occasional, but always welcome, helper in the garden, who generally cut my hedges for me, was Douglas, the eldest son of the farmer, then a lad of about fifteen. Long-faced, with twinkling grey eyes and loosely built, he was happily free from inhibitions, talking freely of his joys and sorrows as he clipped away at the hedge. He generally wore a very old tweed coat, rather long for him, corduroy breeches and leggings with a soft felt hat, pulled well over the back of his head, that had long since lost its band and all semblance of its original shape, or colour, taking on the elemental form that belonged to the country way of life before the day of fashions. A hard worker, keen on learning every detail of his trade, he probably already knew more about it than many farmers twice his age. At that time, when tractors were unknown in the Cotswolds, horses were indispensable in farming, even oxen being still used on a few out-of-the-way hill farms, and Douglas was passionately fond of horses. I noted down, after he had gone home, one little story he told me, describing his fondness for a pony, and now give it as near as I could remember at the time, just as he told me: "It was always Major then, Sir, for me! Why, after a day's threshing and a big supper I did often holler out 'Major' in my sleep, that loud it did wake the other boys up—I was fair mad on that little horse! You see, Sir, he was one as I broke myself and then nobody couldn't manage him but I, and that somehow made I like 'im. Why, I've known the time off'en when he's run right along the stable as straight as a hare under the noses of the other horses and out of the door. Carter did never tie 'un up. It was enough for he to get 'im into 'is place, but I didn't never tie 'im till Carter had gone, lest he'd give him a stroke or two. Many a happy day have I spent behind that little horse at drag or at plough—and I always had 'im, too, ever since he ran away with young Kelly—Ah, he was that artful you never knew what artful dodge he'd be up to next. You had to be watching him all the time to see what he'd be up to. Not like some on 'em, when you might as well go to sleep for all they'd do. Sometimes the old parson'd give I a tanner, or I'd earn a penny choppin' wood, or summat, but it all went to buy ribbons for Major! Then if it we' Market Day I'd pleat up his mane and his tail with straw and ribbon and give 'im ɐ good groomin', and you can take my word, he did look smart! I reckon that's how I lost him in the end, for Dad, he sold him to some toff one Market Day. When he told I, I could have set and cried, I was that fond of the little horse. I must ha' looked a bit queer like, for Dad said, 'Why, what's up, Douglas?' and I said, 'Dad, I'd sooner you done anything than sold Major—you always sells the animals as I likes best.' But Dad never said nothing, he just walked away."

114

Douglas served right through the 1914-18 war, getting married soon after his return, when his father bought him a farm about ten miles away. I occasionally see him on market days at Cirencester. Of course, he drives a car now, but it isn't a very smart one—"a farmer can't do without a car nowadays." He has put on a lot of weight, too, but when he smiles there is something of the same twinkle in his eyes as there used to be when he told me of Major's artful tricks all those years ago.

Those first few months of married life were very happy ones. Ernest Barnsley had started his magnum opus, Rodmarton Manor, and I helped him with its superintendence. The house was built in a leisurely way, taking several years to complete, but this was all to the good, as it allowed time for the converting and seasoning of the timber, all of which was obtained from the local woods. It must have been the last house of its size to be built in this way and probably the last time timber was sawn on the pit in this country. Rodmarton was only four miles away, so he and I often walked over across Tarlton Downs, not always taking the most direct route, as he liked to bring back a good supply of mushrooms when possible. At other times I worked for Gimson, while I was beginning to have a certain amount of work on my own account, but there wasn't really enough to keep me fully occupied, so I was glad to take the opportunity to superintend the repair of the Great Tower at Magdalen College, Oxford, when the work was offered to me. We spent about six months at Oxford, finding lodgings beyond Magdalen Bridge. The work on the tower was interesting though not easy, owing to the depth of decay of the Headington Stone with which the tower was faced. While Magdalen is one of, if not quite, the most beautiful of the Oxford Colleges, I found it also extremely hospitable. Some of the dons took a great interest in the work and at their invitation I was privileged to dine at the high table several times. The President also invited me to the annual Gaude Dinner, when many distinguished visitors are present and there are many toasts and speeches. The choir sang grace from the gallery over the richly carved Tudor screen, after which a great silver loving cup is passed round, containing a delicious liquor, the recipe of which is a closely guarded secret of the college. Dining at Magdalen is (or was then) occasionally rather embarrassing owing to the hospitable custom in which if any of the dons invite you to drink with him you must always empty your glass, but fortunately my previous education at the other university had provided me with a fairly strong head. One of the Fellows of the college at that time was the charming and witty Sir Walter Raleigh, who, judging from his *Lines Written at a Garden Party*, must have been a past master at the art of hiding his feelings! I was also asked to dine at Balliol, where I had a little work to do at the Chapel. Having been an undergraduate myself not so many years ago (though not at Balliol), dining at the high table among the learned and distinguished ones, so isolated on the high dais from the noisy undergraduates in the body of the Hall below, was to me at first an almost eerie experience, "as of an interloper among the Olympian Gods, as they lie beside their nectar." However, this sensation soon wore off, thanks perhaps to that same nectar of many excellent vintages from their well-stocked college cellars. The Prince of Wales, afterwards King Edward VIII, came up for a year at Magdalen at this time and I had to superintend the alterations and redecorations of the rooms he was to occupy. After he came up I often used to see him crossing the Quad when I was working on the tower.

He was popular with the other undergraduates, making his friends from among all classes. In the peculiar jargon fashionable among them at the time, he was known as The Pragger Wagger. Anxious as he was to be indistinguishable from other undergraduates, he insisted on riding an ordinary push-bike, rather to the regret of Dr. Warren, the President, who thought it was beneath his dignity.

One day when I was on the tower, a message came that I was wanted at once. When I reached the gateway I found my wife and her younger sister, who was staying with us, wet through to the skin. They had been out punting on the Cher and had both fallen in—one in a vain attempt to help the other—but luckily had been able to get to the bank and climb out. So I had to find a cab and bribe the cabman to take them home and fortunately they were none the worse for the adventure. We spent many pleasant summer evenings on the Cher, punting or canoeing and there were no more accidents. We also went to Henley Regatta and explored the country round on bicycles, a pleasant enough way of doing so in those days. Oxford was then a much smaller and quieter city, with no traffic problems. Mr. Morris may have been making his first experimental car in a small workshop in the town, but there were no large factories or housing suburbs for the workers in them. There was a song of the period shewing the attitude of ordinary country folk to motoring, which begins:

"The rich folk go by in their madcap machinery;
They kicks up the dust and they spoils all the
    greenery,"
but cars were still so comparatively rare that one could cycle for miles along main country roads without meeting one, though, the roads being still untarred, when one did meet a car one got smothered in dust in dry weather.

117

Though we enjoyed our Oxford experiences, we were glad to get back to Sapperton, to take up much the same sort of life as before. Friends came to stay with us and the Barnsleys throughout most of the summer months, so there were plenty of picnics and excursions to join in. A favourite afternoon excursion was to walk to the Ten Rides in Oakley Park and on to the Wood House for an excellent tea with some of the Welsh cheesecakes for which Mrs. Neil, the headkeeper's wife, was locally famous. Close by was the sham ruin known as King Alfred's Hall, which in spite of fourteenth century windows and a seventeenth century open fireplace "where the cakes were burnt" was credited with having taken in many eighteenth century antiquaries!

There were also some white peacocks to add a touch of exotic splendour to the scene. Another pleasant afternoon could be spent in a walk through Hailey Wood to Tunnel House, where we could have a game of skittles and have tea in the spacious bay-ended room over the bar. There were plenty of pleasant walks to take with our friends, while we could generally borrow bicycles for them for longer excursions, such as to Painswick, to see the wonderful churchyard with its 99 clipped yew trees and the picturesque houses and cottages in that village. Mr. Seddon, the parson there, was a bit of a character himself, and very popular with his parishioners. He told us a story of an old pensioner who had been a regular churchgoer, but stayed away when collections were started. When Seddon took him to task about this, telling him that he ought to be glad to give his last penny to Jesus Christ, the old man retorted, "Ah, so I would if I thought he'd get it." Another excursion was to the ruined castle of Beverstone, not many miles beyond Tetbury and a few miles further on to Owlpen, a very beautiful and romantically situated old house, which had been deserted by its owners for a new mansion about a mile away about a century before. The house was rapidly falling into complete decay, but a caretaker lived in a kitchen wing and would shew some of the rooms to visitors, including one the walls of which were hung with painted canvas, of the kind Falstaff recommended to Dame Quickly. The terraced gardens with a yew parlour and groups of great clipped yews remained just as they were in the time of Queen Anne, a gardener being kept to look after them. There was also a large barn containing a cider mill and a massive oak cider press, as well as the old mill of the manor, which had been kept in tolerable repair, as the mill wheel

OWLPEN MANOR etching by F.L. GRIGGS

119

was used to pump water up to the modern house. In spite of the dilapidation of the house, which was so far advanced that one of the main roof trusses had given way, the great stone bay window had become almost detached from the wall and huge roots of ivy had grown right across some of the floors, it seemed to me that such an exceptionally beautiful and interesting old house might still be saved. However, the owner at that time did not wish either to sell it or to repair it herself. Some years later, when the old lady who had owned it died, the new owner put the property up for auction, so I was able to buy the old manor house, with seven acres of garden and woodland, and put it in repair, though I could not afford to live in it myself. A few of the farms near Owlpen made Double Gloucester cheese, so we generally brought some back with us when we went there. Nearby, too, above Uley, was a large Romano-British camp from which there were extensive views towards and beyond Dursley, while at the top of the hill was a famous Neolithic long barrow, to enter which you could obtain the key and a candle from the farm nearby. The next village bore the romantic name of Nymphsfield!

A Spring excursion was to Kempley, in the Severn Valley, to see the little Norman church with its remarkable frescoes, the churchyard and meadows round it full of wild daffodils. A much shorter one was to Oaksey to see the fields of snakeshead fritillaries. We also took most of our visitors to see the famous windows in Fairford church, Bibury and the Coln Valley, and the archæologically-inclined to the Roman villa at Chedworth.

At Bibury, besides the near-perfect village and the hospitable Swan Hotel, there was Arthur Severn's trout farm. There was also an enormous trout living under the bridge, the sight of which lured many

fishermen to stay at the Swan. But he was too cunning
to be caught and being also a cannibal had eaten all
the other trout in that part of the Coln, so those who
came fished in vain. Eventually he was shot and the
stream re-stocked.

I could go on for many pages describing the many
places of beauty and interest within easy reach of
Sapperton. Many of our friends were so well satisfied
with the village and its immediate surroundings that they
had no desire to go further afield, and with more than
forty years' experience I myself can never tire of it.

Soon after we got back from Oxford, Will Rothenstein, the artist (later Sir William), bought Iles Farm
at Oakridge and employed me as his architect for
alterations and repairs to the house. It was a long
narrow house with a yard immediately beyond it, on
the other side of which was a barn with a side wall
leaning over so much that it was nearly two feet out of
the perpendicular. A wing was added to the house at
the back of the yard, with an open loggia leading to the
barn, which was to be Rothenstein's studio. Much of
the barn had to be re-built and some alterations made
in the house itself, while the yard was paved round
formally arranged rose-beds to form a forecourt.
Arthur Gardiner, the Sapperton carpenter, acted as
builder, all the masons, stone tilers and carpenter being
Oakridge men. Rothenstein suggested that one of
Gimson's blacksmith's apprentices who lived at Oakridge should make the latches, hinges, casements and
other ironwork required in his spare time, and at first
I saw no harm in this, but when it was pointed out to
me that the man had no workshop of his own and was
making these things in Gimson's workshops, using his
fuel and tools, of course I had to make a different
arrangement, and as Rothenstein would not go to Gimson for them owing to the small extra cost he charged

to cover working expenses, I arranged that they should be made by a smith at Bisley. Unfortunately, I could never get Rothenstein to appreciate the necessity for the change, and many years afterwards in his *Men and Memories* he refers to it in a way that is most unfair to Gimson's memory. In this book he says that "Gimson was averse to doing private work" and accuses him "of withdrawing the capable village blacksmith and carpenter from local occupations to make furniture and ironwork for wealthy men living in distant towns." These charges are both unfair and untrue. As for the first, most of Gimson's work *was* private work. It was what he preferred, and he never refused work from local people, provided they did not attempt to dictate to him, or beat down the price. As for the second charge, it is quite ludicrous. He withdrew no skilled blacksmiths or carpenters from local occupations. On the contrary, he took village youths as apprentices and trained them, afterwards employing them at better wages that they would otherwise have been able to command. There were plenty of blacksmiths and carpenters in the district for Rothenstein to employ if he wanted to, but—and this was the crux of the matter—they had not been trained by Gimson. I hope I have said enough about this to clear Gimson's name from the aspersions cast on it in Rothenstein's book. Both men are, alas, dead, but I have tried to do what I can to leave on record a refutation of the charge, lest in the future readers of *Men and Memories* may accept Rothenstein's version of the disagreement.

There was no actual quarrel between them. Gimson never quarrelled with anyone, as far as I know. He just made his position clear and left it at that, bearing no rancour against anyone who differed from him. Needless to say, he remained my friend as much as ever. As for Rothenstein, he was a very likeable man in many ways, and his family was charming. Naturally, I was over there a great deal while the work to the house was going on, and as a constant stream of celebrities of all kinds came to stay with him to be drawn or painted, I met a number of most interesting people there. Rothenstein had not long been back from an extended tour of India, where he had met and been greatly impressed by the Indian poet, Rabindranath Tagore. When Tagore came to England the following year, he did much to bring his work to public notice. It was much to his credit that he often gave a great deal of his time to furthering the work of hitherto little-known artists and writers, whose work in his opinion deserved recognition, and he was particularly generous in this way to many young men who might otherwise have had to wait much longer before their work was appreciated. Tagore came for a long visit to Iles Farm and while he was there we were invited with other friends to go over and hear him recite one of his longer poems. He was an impressive, if a shade theatrical, figure in his Eastern robes, as he read his poem in perfect English, by moonlight on the terrace in front of the house. On another occasion John Drinkwater was prevailed upon to read some of his works—but not by moonlight!

From 1914 to 1918 Max Beerholm lived in a cottage at Far Oakridge belonging to Sir William (then 'Will') Rothenstein, quite close to his home, Iles Farm. For part of that time I was altering Iles Farm for Rothenstein, and being very friendly with him and his charming family, I was over there a great deal. Max spent much of his time at Iles Farm, as **W.R.** was one of his oldest friends, and he was devoted to the children, so it was my great good fortune to see him frequently while he was there. At first it amazed me to see him, in the depths of the country, in war time, always perfectly groomed and immaculately dressed as if for a garden party at Buckingham Palace, but as I got to know him better I realised that he just could not do anything else. In country tweeds he would have felt ridiculous and uncomfortable, even his spats were an essential part of him! There seemed to be a kind of imperturbable perfection, or perhaps, urbanity, about him, without the least effort or ostentation. Add to this his conversational gifts, penetrating wit, and the perfection in its own way of his writing and caricatures, and it is not to be wondered at that he had already been called 'The Incomparable Max.'

As for me, at that time I was young and very shy, and would have been more than content to have kept well in the background, listening to the pearls of wit and wisdom that fell from the lips of Max and Will Rothenstein. It was also a novel and particularly welcome experience to meet a celebrity who more than came up to expectations. Previously I had met so many, at Rothenstein's and elsewhere, who had failed to do so, that I had begun to wonder whether feet of clay were not the normal appurtenances of the great! But with Max it was a very different story and besides that he never monopolised the conversation, but with unfailing courtesy and tact drew everyone into the circle, laughed heartily at other people's jokes, even the most elementary, and never appeared to be bored. Being rather addicted to long walks myself, one of his idiosyncrasies that most struck me was his dislike of—even the abhorrence—of walking, declaring that his brain simply went to sleep during a walk, making rational conversation impossible. So far as I know, he never took any exercise for the sake of his health, and perhaps the fact that he lived to be 83 and had very little illness till the last few months of his life, tends to shew that exercise is a much less important factor in health than careful living—the Greek theory of moderation in all things. This reluctance to take exercise he transferred to Rosetti in his caricature of Meredith inviting him to go for a walk and much later in his delightful Radio Sketch of 'Hethway Speaking.'

One anecdote he related surprised me very much, as it showed that even he—the most tactful of men—could slip up occasionally. It was about W. H. Davies, the tramp poet who came back from America having lost a leg jumping off a train there. He was at that time in very poor circumstances and a number of influential people who admired his work clubbed together to help him. Bernard Shaw, who had done a great deal of work in getting subscriptions, and had given liberally himself, took the chair at the dinner given to present the money collected to Davies. Max, who had not expected to be called upon, was asked to speak, and remarked that this wasn't the first time that Shaw had helped a lame dog over a stile. Davies, morbidly sensitive about his disability, and, white with anger, turned his back on Max, and refused to listen to any explanations. He did not refuse the money, but he said something bitter in his speech in accepting it, about kicking a man when he was down.

All this was, very naturally, very painful to Max, as in his use of the cliche, he had of course, been thinking only of Shaw's generosity, and not at all of poor Davies' misfortune, but the damage was done and Davies never forgave him. One of the things that particularly impressed me about Max was his great tact and consideration for others' feelings, and I remember feeling, when he told the story, that if *he* could unintentionally pass such a brick, there was little hope for the rest of us!

One day he described how when some years previously he had had a bad attack of neuralgia, he had persuaded his doctor to give him an injection of morphia. In the dream that followed, he saw an endless procession of tiny men, about a foot high, all exactly alike, and dressed in black frock coat, pepper and salt trousers, spats, etc. of the man-about-town of that period, each one, as he slowly moved past him, squinting at him over his shoulder.   He said, and I could well believe him, that of the two evils, he preferred neuralgia, and he had taken a vow never to have morphia again.   Another anecdote was of burning a book—one left in the cottage by some previous occupant—the cottage had previously been let, and in some cases, lent, to a number of Rothenstein's friends and acquaintances, including Dr. Herringham and John Drinkwater, and no doubt some of these visitors had left books behind them which they probably never expected, or wanted, to see again.   At any rate, there was this book on the bookshelf, and one miserably cold, wet winter's day, being alone, and not having anything else he wanted to do, Max took it down and started to read it. But alas, it was such dreadful tripe that he found it utterly unreadable, and consumed with righteous fury he threw it into the fire. The fireplace was one of those utterly inefficient cottage ranges with a small open fire in the middle, between an inadequate oven and what was known, quite properly, as a sham on the other side. Most of the heat went up the chimney, and the fire generally smoked, and in such a day as Max described, it was probably at its worst. However, at first the unaccustomed fuel produced some improvement. Bright flames started up, but very soon died down after the few outside pages had been burnt. Only by constant poking could the inner pages be induced to burn a little at a time, meanwhile the fire became more and more choked with charred paper. The book took a long time to burn and all the time Max suffered qualms of conscience, for after all, he accused himself, it wasn't *his* book, and he had no right

126

to burn it. Suppose someone came in and saw it burning, what excuse could he make, and so on. In the end, he was left with a grate full of charred paper, a few dead coals, and some still triumphant remains of unburnt book. There was nobody he could call in to clear away the mess and make a new fire. Outside it was snowing, and in any case Rothenstein and his family were away for a few days. So he had to clear up the grate and find the materials for a new fire and make it himself—a thing he had never had to do in his life, and it was not till after several attempts (what with wet wood, damp paper and other drawbacks) that he got the fire going at last.

I have given the bare bones of these anecdotes as best I could remember them, but how differently Max told them, anyone who knew him would appreciate! His eloquent gestures, his delightfully modulated voice, low but distinct, capable of the utmost pathos or the most jubilant gaiety, and above all, his choice of words and phrases—inimitable indeed!

To the Rothenstein children he was an adored 'uncle.' He drew for them, played with them, wrote poems about their pets. There was one about Rover, their large retriever, a most affectionate and much loved animal in reality, but in the poem the most murderous of creatures, who slaughtered one by one the whole family, besides two uncles, a goat whose ghost haunted him ever after, and all the children!

Towards the end of his stay, we were invited to an unofficial exhibition in the cottage of the drawings he had made for 'Rosetti and his Circle' which had been drawn during his stay there. What a feast it was! Besides the cartoons later published in the book were a few daring but extremely witty ones relating to the Royal Family. These were considered by some to be too near the borderline of lèse majesté, so they were afterwards withdrawn.

Poor Max felt the cold very much during the winters he spent at Oakridge. How glad he must have been to exchange the climate of the 'Cold Cotswolds' for that of his beloved Italy, when the war ended and he was able to return there.

I never saw him again, only renewing his acquaintance in his books, and then in listening to his radio sketches, alas only too few.

Lady Rothenstein had a story of him at the time he was staying at Oakridge. She and Mrs. Beerholm were out for a short walk, when a lark got up and started to sing. Mrs. Beerholm said at once that she must hurry back and fetch Max, because he had never heard a lark. But Max took so long finding his right gloves, cane, spats and hat for a country walk, that by the time they reached the field they sought, the lark was no longer to be seen or heard. With his dislike of country walks and of getting his boots muddy, it is probable that he never *did* hear a lark sing.

The episode of burning the book he later used in 'The Crime,' a chapter in 'And Even Now.'

At this time Rothenstein was painting subjects mostly in the immediate neighbourhood, especially the large barns at Oakridge farms and a great wych elm in the meadow in front of his house. At the same time he was making a number of portraits, many of them in pencil. Some of them seemed to me to be good likenesses, others not so good. He made a good portrait of Ernest Barnsley and I acquired a very good one of old Eli Gardiner, the thatcher.

But before the work at Iles Farm was finished the 1914-18 war had begun. For the first year it did not appear to make very much difference to life in the country. There were even placards encouraging "Business as Usual" and many people thought that the enormous cost of a world war would bring it to an end in a matter of months.

However, we were soon undeceived on that score, and when the Derby Group Scheme was published, I volunteered with many others from the neighbourhood, but was rejected on medical grounds, owing to an enlarged heart. I therefore obtained some work in London and had to say good-bye to Sapperton for a while. By the time I came back a new era had dawned.

WORK AT ILES FARM
Alterations undertaken by the author for William Rothenstein

129

Chapter VII

CAMPDEN AND AFTER

IN the last year or two before the First World War and after it till his death in 1938, a great deal of my time was spent at Campden, chiefly on account of my friendship with Fred Griggs, who then lived at Dover's House, a Georgian stone house of great beauty and refinement in Campden High Street. He was at that time a bachelor attended by Minnie, his elderly and devoted housekeeper, who took infinite pride in keeping the felicitously furnished house tidy and spotless, while her cooking was admirable. At this time he was chiefly known for the illustrations he had made for a number of the *Highways and Byways* series of books, in making the drawings, for which he had travelled over much of the country in search of his subjects. His passionate love of England—in particular of England before the Reformation—and of the peaceful beauty of the country untouched by the blight of industrialisation, accentuated by these years of careful observation, study and research, had given him a unique insight into the mediæval architecture and rural aspect of the country at that time and up to the industrial revolution. In consequence his etchings of Gothic churches and monasteries, as well as his imaginary landscapes, although they were entirely his own inventions, appeared to live as actual buildings and scenes, drawn on the spot with the minutest care. Early in his career he had made a few small etchings of subjects in the neighbourhood of Hitchin (his birthplace), but these were in his opinion merely experimental and for several years he put etching on one side while he was engaged on other work. When he first visited Sapperton he had just taken it up again, and for the rest of his life etching

130

F. L. GRIGGS

131

was his chosen medium. With infinite patience and research he mastered the difficult technique until his plates were as superb technically as they were imaginative and beautiful artistically. At this time, however, he had only published a few small plates and his work as an etcher was only beginning to be widely recognised. Apart from his work, which I greatly admired, he had so many human and intellectual qualities which appealed to me that his friendship became more to me than that of anyone, except Ernest Gimson. He had a real knowledge of the best English literature, based on much reading and a retentive memory, a keen appreciation of poetry and love of music. He could play the piano from ear, was an excellent accompanist, delighted in country dancing and old songs, revelled in a joke, could laugh heartily without affectation, enjoyed country sports of all kinds, especially cricket, was a connoisseur of good food and drink and was, in fact, the most delightful companion possible. No wonder then that when I went to Campden, which was frequently, I spent as much time with him as I could, though I had work to do there too, and this was the more easy as I always had to stay the night there, it being impossible to get there and back in a day, before I had a car. At Dover's House I soon got to know almost everyone in Campden interested in the arts, crafts or music, as friends and acquaintances were always dropping in and always hospitably welcomed. One of the things Fred loved most was the sound of church bells, the fine peal of bells in Campden Church tower with their melodious chimes being one of the many reasons that specially drew him to make his home in the town. His interest in bell-ringing led him to give an annual feast to the ringers, with the addition of a few of his personal friends and some local inhabitants notable for geniality and ability to entertain.

132

The ringers themselves were rather shy, or at least reserved, lot of men. They were, of course, officially at any rate, Church of England, and were possibly a little suspicious of being entertained by a Catholic. However, Fred's genius for hospitality very soon broke through this and they enjoyed themselves thoroughly. The feast was held at the Lygon Arms, in a large room normally used for farmers' ordinaries. The landlord, John Skey, whose proportions were a testimonial in themselves to a life-long appreciation of good food and drink, proudly carved the joint, an immense sirloin, tender and juicy, cooked to a turn. I shouldn't wonder if he had not a personal knowledge of the beast, carefully fed and selected, which produced it! At any rate the joint always did him credit and he carved it and presided over its distribution with a solemnity worthy of a great occasion. All the fitting accessories in the way of vegetables and horseradish sauce were there, and the lavish helpings were repeated for all who required them. The sweet course was one of Mrs. Skey's famous pies, with plenty of cream, followed by a ripe old Cheddar or Double Gloucester cheese to round off the simple but ample meal. For drink there was the best draught ale from Stratford-on-Avon in pint mugs and tankards. After toasts to the King, the bells, the host and many others had been dealt with, chairs were drawn back and the air became hazy with tobacco smoke, the tables were cleared except for fresh jugs of beer, and songs were called for. Some of the older men needed a good deal of persuading, but there is no tongue-loosener to compare with beer; and once persuaded, off they started with a few quavery notes, then, warming to it, heartened by the lusty way all joined in the chorus, sang more and more confidently, finishing off beaming amid general applause to reach out for their tankards to quench their well-earned thirst.

Such a one was dear old George Groves, one of the best masons in a village famous for its traditional skill in working the fine local stone, full of quiet wisdom and one of Nature's gentlemen, if there ever was one. One erstwhile music hall comedian had a great ovation for a song almost as broad as it was long—it was a longish song, too—with a rousing chorus beginning "All I wants is good company", but for the most part the faded old songs of two or more generations before were brought out again from the recesses in which they had been stored in the memories of old men who had sung them last perhaps when they were courting "and the golden hair was hanging down her back." Such songs as "The man on the Flying Trapeze" and "Two Little Girls in Blue", some of which are now familiar again through revival on the radio. All the time, Fred was the life and soul of the party; his hearty laugh could be heard as he cracked jokes with all and sundry; he saw that no one went short of drink, or had a chance of feeling "out of it"; he accompanied the songs on the piano, skilfully adapting the key to suit the often limited compass of the singer and vamping tunes he had never come across before merely from hearing the air hummed by the singers. When closing time came and after many hearty Good Nights the company took their several ways home, there were few who did not hope to be invited again the following year.

Nowadays perhaps such an entertainment might be considered tedious and uninteresting, but those were simpler days, and I doubt whether many of those present would have enjoyed anything else half as well. In such things it is the spirit that counts, and in anything where Fred took a leading part no one could fail to respond to his genius for good fellowship.

When I was a boy in the 1890's, there was a picture shop in Norwich, in the window of which works by local artists were shown. These often included small watercolours, and occasionally larger oil paintings by Munnings. I especially remember one of three splendid horses pulling a timber waggon loaded with great tree trunks, the driver walking beside the leading horse up a slight hill bordered by tall elms. I wanted that picture badly, but although the prices asked were not high, they were beyond my means.

There was also a water colour in the picture gallery of the Castle Museum of a corner of a country fair, full of the picturesque characters to be seen at such gatherings at that time. I still go to see it whenever I go to Norwich, giving only a cursory glance at the Great Auk and the Cassoway, among the vast number of stuffed birds and animals that form the greater number of exhibits, before reaching the pictures.

Some twenty years later when I had work as an architect there, the Munnings used to stay at the Noel Arms at Campden, and I soon got to know them through Fred Griggs. They were then and for some years afterwards, looking for a country home, and I sometimes accompanied them to vet. the house in case alterations were needed. One property we looked at, at Kingcombe, didn't appeal to either of them at first. After going round the house, A.J. had dropped behind as we rather listlessly examined the surroundings. Suddenly Violet Munnings started to sniff. 'Alfred,' she called, 'come here quickly, I smell fox. Do you know, I rather like this place.' Alfred, no longer listless, heartily agreed. 'Not at all a bad little place; it has its points.' Such wonders can a scent of fox produce. However, they decided not to buy the property.

At another time he and I inspected a fine old house, traditionally the home of Tyndale, but, when we saw it, in very bad repair. The old farmer was a man after A.J.'s heart, and they had a great time together, swapping

135

yarns. The old man stood in the middle of the yard formed by the house and farm buildings, a great heap of manure beside him, and whistled, bringing pigs galloping from every direction. He pointed out a charming little building in which Tyndale was said to have worked at his translation, but which had since been used for a different purpose, and told us that that very morning, he had had quite a shock when a large rat had jumped out of the hole in the seat! But most of his anecdotes referred to one of his men who had arrived at the farm some five years before, begging for employment and board and lodging. His wife and her lover had threatened to kill him if he didn't leave them in his small farm in Wales, and he was so frightened that he went! He seemed perfectly happy, was an excellent man on the farm, and sang in the church choir, apparently having no wish to return to Wales and claim his property.

We had a most enjoyable day there, but Munnings decided not to buy the house, as the meadows for his horses were on a steep hillside, too dangerous for valuable hunters, so we left the old man with many regrets, taking with us one of his Double Gloucester cheeses, which were still made in his dairy.

Many other farms we visited before A.J. at last found exactly what he wanted in his own county of Suffolk; an old house of character, enough meadow land for his horses and some mature elm trees. Most landscape painters have their favourite trees. For Old Crome the oak, for Cotman the ash, and many of us got tired of Macwhirter's silver birches, but for Munnings, it was the elm above all. He never minded how much trouble he took to get what he wanted. I once went quite a long trip with him to Yarmouth to visit the kilns then bordering the beach, with their hundreds of herrings on hooks, a smouldering oak fire turning them into

Yarmouth kippers. A much quicker and easier way, it was rumoured, with the help of creosote, had already been found to produce kippers, but nothing but the good old method would do for him.

Some people were distressed by his manners. He was the son of a Suffolk miller and never attempted to shed his rough country ways, even in the drawing room. To see him at his best, you had to be with him at an old country inn, with its uneven floor, three legged round topped tables and wide settles, and with a roaring fire in the open fireplace, and the pleasant faint smell of wood smoke. There he was the life and soul of the party, reciting his own poems and singing his own songs to his own tunes—I well remember one occasion when four of us had dinner at the Cheshire Cheese, and afterwards, in a private room, sat round the table, rubbing lumps of sugar on lemons—the first stage of making

---

NOTE

In case any reader would like to sample Munnings' recipe for punch, here it is:—

A pint of rum, a pint of sherry, a pint of brandy, a pound of loaf sugar, each lump being rubbed on the outside of a lemon until well saturated. (Note the delicious aroma of this process). Two or more lemons, according to taste, to be cut in half and squeezed over the sugar in the bowl. A handful of cloves simmering gently on the stove while the rum, brandy and sherry are warming there all together in a saucepan. Then a pint or more, according to taste, are poured over the sugar in the bowl, the clove water being added as well. (Here again, note the aroma)! After stirring with the ladle, pour the warm spirits on and stir again. Then what a glorious bowl of steaming nectar! The very smell alone makes you merry and bright. This recipe has never been known to fail in making a night.

punch according to the recipe he had got from the famous Harleston Inn—and of course, later emptied the bowl. The nine or more verses he recited of 'Brother Hill, He Milketh Yet,' were not too long, nor was his song of his early loves, ending with 'I stood in the puddles with Julia, With Julia ages ago.' Later we took a taxi to his studio in Chelsea where his latest paintings appealed to us more than ever, but seen through something of a golden haze.

What the ultimate verdict on his work will be is a matter for conjecture, but the horses in his pictures are more alive than any that have been painted, except those by his beloved exemplar—Stubbs—or so it seems to me. In his depicting of country characters he came near to Breughel in some of his early work.

As a man, what struck you was his tremendous enthusiasm for what he liked or admired. As his successor to the Presidency of the Royal Academy, Sir Gerald Kelly, said in his obituary notice, 'He had *gusto*, and gusto is a rare and precious quality.'

As I have said, I always stayed the night when I went to Campden, and sometimes the week-end, generally putting up either at the Lygon Arms or at the Dunn's. These were a real old Campden couple, both of them belonging to families who had been established there for many generations. Mrs. Dunn, a woman of forcible character, was the daughter of William Haynes, a plumber and coppersmith, over whose shop hung as a sign an enormous copper kettle. He was long since dead at this time, but the sign was still there. Like many of the old Campden folk he had clung to old customs long after they had died out elsewhere, and she told me that when she was a child the family still used pewter plates, cleaning them with elder twigs. When she grew up she became a schoolmistress, travelling as far as the Hebrides to learn and so be able to teach hand-weaving and the spinning and dyeing of wool. Later on she came back to Campden, where she married Dicky Dunn, a gentle and submissive little man with very little to say for himself in the presence of his masterful wife, although her sharp tongue had a kind heart behind it, and she was fonder of him than appearances suggested. He was a maltster, no doubt a profitable trade at the time of their marriage, as there were then many inns in Campden that brewed their own beer, and some of the local farmers did so, too, but by the time I knew the Dunns there had been some change in the licensing laws which had obliged him to give up malting. He now spent most of his time standing, a pathetic little figure, under the archway in the High Street which led to his cottage and malthouse, passing the time of day to acquaintances, hoping one of them would have time to stop for a chat. Over his head still hung the sign with his name and trade in now faded letters and with the word "licensed" crossed out:

RICHARD DUNN
~~LICENSED~~
MALTSTER

His grandfather had driven a stage coach and he still had his top coat with its many capes in almost imperishable box cloth. Dicky had been proud of his trade, and though he did not complain it was easy to see how he missed it. Very occasionally he still made a little malt for a farmer and he couldn't conceal his pleasure in shewing me how it was done, on one of these occasions. When his wife was not about he liked to talk of his early days. "When I was a bit of a lad," he would say, "I used to like being sent up to

139

Hinchwick (a mansion about four miles from Campden)—that was when General Lygon lived there—to take a message or something. It didn't matter who it was, as soon as the door was opened, the butler, a big, fat, smiling man he was, would say, 'Well, my boy, what'll you have, smalls, middleboy or routemstoutem?' Smalls was a very good small beer, what you'd call light ale, middleboy was a better beer than you get in Campden to-day, but routemstoutem—that *was* some stuff! You didn't want much of that—that is if you had to walk home again;" I asked him which he chose. "Well, he said, "I generally had middleboy. I did have routenstoutem once though, but I didn't get home that night! Lord, how they laughed the next time I went there when I told them I'd spent the night in the ditch. Dear me, no, they don't brew their own beer at Hinchwick now. Haven't done for forty years, I expect. That was in General Lygon's time, that was. Yes, the Lygon Arms is because of the General—very much liked he was—a proper gentleman," and so on! Campden had been an important town until the decline of the wool trade, since when it had gradually declined to becoming merely an agricultural centre. Owing also to its being well away from main roads leading to the large towns, with even its railway station a mile away, it was a very self-centred place, very little affected by the changes caused by industrialisation. Its inhabitants didn't mind being considered old-fashioned; they preferred the old fashions! This conservatism of outlook applied to the greater part of the Cotswolds up to the time of the First World War, but was especially characteristic of Campden. They loved and were proud of their old town with its ancient traditions, much resenting any attempt at interference by outsiders from Birmingham and such places, who told them they were behind the times and tried to "wake them up". Also they didn't think very highly of such occasional visitors who admired the old place as a sort of museum piece, but knew nothing of the old country way of life or the traditional skilled country crafts that were such an essential part of it. Fred and I, it is needless to say, entirely appreciated the Campden point of view, enjoying the comments of some of the older inhabitants about these gentry. There was Phillip Merriman, an old farm labourer, who, as a young man, was one of six Campden men who made an annual trip to London, to mow the lawns of Campden House at Kensington. He was a whimsical old fellow, full of country lore, who was such a favourite of Fred's that he dedicated one of his early plates to him. One of his remarks was, "Well, I likes eddicated people, but the wust on't is they be so domned ignorant"—a remark containing more intrinsic wisdom than may appear at first sight! Then there was an old man at Ebrington, a neighbouring village, who was buttonholed in the village street by a sightseer full of gush about the quaintness of its thatched cottages. His retort was, "Yes, I desay it's a quaint old place—and we gets some quaint people come to look at it, too". Along with old prejudices, old superstitions lingered on too, and it was on account of one of them that some of the old people held me responsible, albeit unwittingly, for the death of one man and the frightening of several others! It happened in this way. I was called in as architect to advise on the condition of the chancel arch of the church. Several alarming cracks were visible which, though they had been there as long as anyone could remember, the new vicar decided to have remedied. As one of the piers is very close to the Gainsborough family vault, I suggested that it was advisable to examine the vault in case there had been any subsidence causing a settlement of the pier. So, permission to

141

open the vault having been obtained from Lord Gainsborough, who sent his agent down to represent him, a
mason made the necessary preparations to expose the
steps leading down into it and the vicar, Lord Gainsborough's agent, the sexton and I started to go down.
The vicar and the agent had already disappeared into
the vault when Harry Withers, the sexton, pulled me
by the sleeve as I was starting to follow them. I was
surprised that he had turned quite white and was
trembling. "You know what they say, Sir?" he said.

"No, what is it?" said I, not being able to guess
who or to what he was referring.

"They says as one of us four will be dead within a
week, Sir."

"Well, it's too late to bother about that now, I must
go down, but you stay here if you'd rather."

"Oh no, Sir, I must go too, but I thought I'd better
tell you."

So we joined the others in the vault, which was about
12 feet square, the side walls about five feet high to
the springing of the simple barrel vault, both walls and
vault being of dressed stone accurately fitted. It was
a fine piece of mason's work, the large number of
stones bearing mason's marks shewing that the men
who had built it were proud of their handiwork. After
a careful examination of the walls and vault for any
sign of subsidence, of which there was no sign whatever, we glanced at the coffins, the last of which had
been placed there nearly 200 years before. There were,
I think, three large coffins of lead on which were cast
the family coat-of-arms surmounted by skulls and
breasts of skeletons, one of these lead coffins being
Lady Juliana's. There were also two oak coffins
ornamented with patterns in copper nail heads, and
several tiny coffins, some in lead, presumably of still-
born babies. In a corner there was a grisly heap of

142

bones and decayed pieces of oak coffins. On the inside of the door was pencilled "Lady Juliana's coffin resealed. 1881. W. Haynes." After a hurried glance at all this we climbed back into the comparatively fresh air of the south aisle and were glad to be able to breathe more freely. Three of us were about the same age, between 50 and 60, while I was considerably younger. All appeared to be in reasonably good health, but whether it was a coincidence or not, the agent was taken ill next day, dying two days later, and the sexton was ever afterwards convinced that if we hadn't gone down into that vault he'd have been with us still. And that wasn't the end of the horrid affair. The tenants of the gate-house cottages, just beyond the churchyard, declared that Lady Juliana's ghost was to be seen walking up and down the drive to the ruins of the great house that night and for weeks afterwards "and she'd been quiet ever since her coffin was re-sealed in 1881."

The Lady Juliana mentioned in this story was the only daughter and heiress of Sir Baptist Hicks, afterwards first Viscount Campden, who gave the town its market hall and the splendid row of almshouses that is as fine an example of Cotswold mason's craftsmanship as can be seen anywhere, besides many other benefactions. The mansion that he built in 1612 was said to have been very magnificent, but it was destroyed by fire during the Civil War, not enough of its walls now remaining to give an adequate idea of its former splendour. A charming stone pavilion still remains and another small building, called the Guest House, with the gateway near the churchyard, and Lady Juliana's Gateway on the opposite side of what was the garden enclosure. Lady Juliana married Lord Edward Noel, who became the second Viscount Campden, and from them the present Earl of Gainsborough is descended. Their effigies in marble are in the church, as is that of their daughter Penelope. Lady Juliana lived to the great age of 95 and it was her steward, William Harrison, whose adventures give rise to the mystery known as the Campden Wonder.

Campden was also famous for the Cotswold Games, founded by Robert Dover, with the help at court of his friend Endymion Porter, Groom of the Bedchamber to James I, who procured for his use on opening the Games a suit of the King's clothes, with a feathered hat. The Games were held on Dover's Hill, just above the town. They were prohibited in Cromwell's time, but started again at the Restoration, lasting till 1851, when they were finally suppressed owing to the scandal created by the behaviour of gangs of riffraff from Birmingham and the Black Country, who came by train in thousands, perhaps one of the reasons why the local inhabitants do not think too highly of visitors from Birmingham. The Games, including horse racing, probably took place over an extensive area of what was then unenclosed sheep down, but the focal point was what is now known as Dover's Hill, a fairly level plateau on the top of a convex ridge rapidly sloping down to Aston-Sub-Edge, where Endymion Porter had his seat. This grassy plateau dotted with ancient hawthorns and some 800 feet high, commands a magnificent view across Worcestershire to the Shropshire hills. The slope below it is thickly wooded and the whole area is a noble piece of unspoilt English country which can have changed but little since John Dover founded the Games in 1604, or thereabouts. When it was put up for auction, it was Fred Griggs who succeeded in getting Dover's Hill bought for the National Trust, with the object of preserving the ancient comeliness of the town he loved so well, but perhaps what strikes every visitor to Campden most, of what he has done in Campden, is the noble War

Memorial Cross, and after this the felicitous series of signs, with their graceful ironwork.

Some of the incidents mentioned in this chapter, as well as one or two in the earlier ones, happened after 1918, but as I have already stated, my aim has been, as far as possible, to stop short at the First World War. The reason is sufficiently obvious. Up to that time mechanisation had little affected the countryside, particularly in the Cotswolds, and there still seemed some grounds for hoping that natural beauty, seemly buildings and the handicrafts, even though they were ousted from the larger towns, might still be allowed to exist in the country. True, all these had been losing ground steadily ever since the days of William Morris, but Rural England still remained some sort of stronghold of the traditional way of life. They were good days, or so they seem to me, looking back on them. Life was simpler when Fascism and Communism had not been invented and when "every boy and every girl that's born into this world alive, is either a little Liberal or else a little Conservative", as the song in *Iolanthe* put it. We deplored the factories and the reckless industrialisation which produced the Black Country, and pitied the factory workers. Now factories seem to be considered a panacea and a town without factories pitiable! Only the other day I had a letter from my daughter, quoting a conversation with a gardener at Canterbury about war damage to the cathedral. He said, "Pity Hitler didn't do the job properly and blow the whole cathedral up."

"But why?"

"Why! why then we could have some factories in the town; they won't allow any factories because of the cathedral. Canterbury is all for the artistocracy."

I suppose, in coining that remarkable word, he had in mind the decreasing number of people in this country who can still appreciate the heritage of beauty which past ages have bequeathed to us and a civilised way of life now apparently lost for ever. "What folly," as Ernest Gimson once said, "to exchange two thousand years' of experience for less than two hundred of experiment."

146